GIRLS WITH SOLE

TIME TO **ROCK** YOUR WORLD!

A GIRL POWER GUIDE TO UNLEASHING YOUR INNER SUPERHERO

LIZ FERRO

DEDICATED TO MY DAUGHTER, MORGAN

GIRLS WITH SOLE

A Girl Power Guide to Unleashing Your Inner Superhero

WRITTEN BY
Liz Ferro

Published by:
Library Tales Publishing
www.LibraryTalesPublishing.com
www.Facebook.com/LibraryTalesPublishing

Copyright © 2018 by Liz Ferro
All Rights Reserved
ISBN: 978-1-732888807
Published by Library Tales Publishing
New York, New York

Back cover photograph by Lydia Kearney Carlis.

For general information on our other products and services, please contact our Customer Care Department at 1-800-754-5016, or fax 917-463-0892. For technical support, please visit www.LibraryTalesPublishing.com

Library Tales Publishing also publishes its books in a variety of electronic formats. Every content that appears in print is available in electronic books.

PRINTED IN THE UNITED STATES OF AMERICA

TABLE OF CONTENTS

FOREWORD

From the cushy seats of the Cinemark Valley View movie theater, outside of Cleveland, Ohio, I was watching my name roll on the credits for the blockbuster film, *The Avengers*. I wasn't an actress, but my connections in the film industry and work as a television broadcaster landed me a small role as a news reporter in the superhero franchise. It was only several weeks later that I found myself cocooned in a fetal position underneath the windowsill of my trendy apartment, whispering the words, *"I have nothing."*

My profession, my relationship, my health, and my future all seemed lost. It was the perfect recipe for giving up and surrendering to failure. But even in moments of extreme uncertainty, we can choose not to quit. We can overpower self-pity and weakness, reach into our bag of tricks, and pull out resilience and empowerment. My formula started with my earbuds, a playlist, and Eminem. Eminem was telling me to lose myself in the music, in the moment, and to own it! And so, I ran and put all my emotion out on the pavement and into the air that filled my lungs. It was during this journey of living my playlist when I truly began to appreciate the stories of other women with bold stories to tell.

I remember the first time I met Liz Ferro. It was years before my fallen moment. She was a guest on my talk show at the NBC television station in Cleveland. Liz is small in stature, but her message is loud and strong. In a spirited and honest delivery, Liz talked about her mission to change the lives of young women with the very tool I would one day seek -- empowerment! Through her non-profit organization, Girls with Sole, Liz provides free fitness and wellness programs to help girls empower themselves through their most difficult challenges and life experiences. It's a mission that I believe in because I also experienced how fitness and self-care changed my life. I've spent over two decades interviewing people about their life's work and passions. There's something different, something special, something destined about Liz and her mission. Many people spend their lives searching for their purpose. I know, through my personal conversations with Liz, that saving the lives of young women through Girls with Sole is her purpose. You can hear the commitment and love in Liz's voice when she talks about the young lives she affects through her work; she cheers for them, she cries for them, she empowers them, and she understands their struggles and journey. Liz has walked their path, and she leads by example. Her words and actions change the lives of young women, but also inspire and resonate with women of all ages. Liz is a real-life superhero.

If you're reading *Girls with Sole*, you've either been impacted by Liz Ferro's message, heard about the life-changing moments she creates, or you're ready to make the shift you need for an empowering life! In her raw and witty, yet compassionate voice, Liz guides you through a journey toward self-improvement with workbook exercises that are specific to you. Each chapter is designed for you to take part in self-reflection and discover the tools you need to succeed! Liz's book is a modern-day workbook retreat for your soul. *Girls with Sole* will help you dig a little deeper to find your own groove, step into your own one-woman revolution, and rock out to the happy life you're on a mission to live!

Andrea Vecchio
Emmy-Nominated Television Broadcaster
Author, *Live Your Playlist*

INTRODUCTION

I'm the kind of person who loves workbooks. Something about them makes me feel like my inner child can come out to play in a safe space while creating an at-a-glance treasury of memories I can flip through and enjoy for years to come.

I do realize that not everyone shares my zest and zeal for workbooks - or even workouts, for that matter. They are heavy words - words we feel we need a strength we don't already possess in order to mess with.

What if the words 'workbook' and 'workout' didn't have the word 'work' in them? What if we changed our perspective about making inner changes or changes in our health (mind, body and soul) by eliminating the work and, therefore, no longer viewing the process as painful or difficult? Maybe instead, we could look at it like a party or an adventure - or even a rock concert. Sure, all of these things can come with their own set of challenges, efforts, discomforts or difficulties... but because they kick ass and are fun, we consider them to be worth it! Well, I know for a fact that you're worth it and kick ass - and I'm betting you know you are as well, or you wouldn't have gotten this far on your adventure. (See how awesome this is when you look at it the right way?)

When I think about rock - or rock and roll music - a word that comes to mind is revolution. Revolution has more than one meaning, but I like to think of it as a huge change in thinking and behavior. For instance, rock music changed the world and the way people viewed music, so it was a major revolution. So, if a revolution is a huge change in thinking and behavior, I'd like every one of us to think of ourselves as a one-woman revolution!

We can change the way the world and society view us as women and as female athletes... but more importantly... how we view ourselves.

By using our strength and fitness (mentally, emotionally and physically), we can expand opportunities for ourselves and others and rock out our lives, no matter what obstacles we may face.

The key is focusing on our abilities, finding something we're passionate about, gaining confidence from it, and letting that confidence spill into all the other areas of our lives. This isn't always easy to do. It takes hard work and courage to uncover our true rock-star potential. I would dare to say that it can even be scary to delve into the dive bar corners of our own mind. We want the world to see us as a Ritz Carlton - but often in our own minds, we feel more like a Motel 6.

I think it often boils down to three things: challenge, passion and change. Challenging ourselves both mentally and physically (as well as challenges or trauma we experience in our lives) is key to becoming a one-woman revolution. We need to get good and uncomfortable in order to grow and change. This will also often lead to discovering our passions. Finding what makes your soul sing and chasing your passions will determine the necessary changes needed to actually reach your goals and unleash your badass superpowers. This may mean changing the way you currently do things, the people you surround yourself with, and the way you speak to yourself in your own head.

So, three very basic - but not exactly simple - things can be the difference between you metaphorically headlining a local county rib burn-off festival or selling out the Madison Square Garden of your life - and they are challenge, passion, and change.

A one-woman revolution shows up every day with

two things: attitude and effort. As we all know, sometimes it's our attitudes that need a little effort - but we move forward relentlessly.

Many believed that I was a lost cause for most of my life. Foster care, adoption, and childhood sexual abuse led to self-destructive behaviors for quite a while. So often I wanted someone to save me. Honestly, when I discovered how fitness and wellness helped me tap into the challenge, passion and change that I mentioned earlier, I realized that I needed to be my own hero and save myself by becoming my own one-woman revolution. A one-woman revolution doesn't need anyone to save her. She saves herself. (Capes optional.)

If it weren't for swimming, biking and running, I wouldn't be here to tell you that. Statistically speaking, I shouldn't be here at all. I should be in jail, addicted to drugs or alcohol, or even dead. Everything good in my life is connected in some way to running and fitness. Everything.

It was in challenging my body, setting big goals in my mind and passionately going after them that I got stronger emotionally, built self-esteem and learned that I had what I needed inside of me to recognize and reclaim my power and realize how much I rocked!

This is exactly what Girls with Sole does for the girls we serve! My non-profit, Girls with Sole, developed organically from my personal experiences, now serves as a way to expand opportunities for girls in our programs to realize how much they rock and to Lace Up for a Lifetime of Achievement. We believe in them so that they may believe in themselves.

So, this book is about change. It's not about changing who you are - but instead - making sure you are the best possible version of yourself and giving yourself permission to unleash your inner superhero. It's about developing and growing and being honest with yourself about who you are and who you want to be.

When I run, every step I take changes me. The same is true for people who lift weights, circuit train, dance, swim, ride, walk, box, cross-fit or do yoga. You are transformed into a different person with every stride, set, or pose. The beautiful part about these adventures, parties and rock concerts (all of these create joy, sweat and a sense of well-being) is that you're never exactly the same person you were when you started them - as when you complete them - because your inner self is renewed, reinvented and rejuvenated. Maybe you feel high... like you climbed a mountain (adventurer), danced with your crush (party) or kicked ass and kick-started your mojo with an energy that feels like you could rock out for hours (rock concert).

So, let the adventurer, the rock star and the rebel hero inside of you come out to play and create your own style of health and happiness. It's not work. It's adventure, energy, change, development and growth - and you deserve it. It's about time the world recognized what we already know at Girls with Sole — which is: girls, women and female athletes ROCK!

The rewards of fitness and wellness can be all yours— and just as no one can earn them for you—no one can take them away from you once you achieve them. Accomplishing something you didn't think you could can bring an enormous sense of power and peace. When you find your power and your peace, you'll find your freedom. Nothin' rocks harder than that, dude.

By answering some thought-provoking questions, moving your body, and completing self-awareness building activities - you will soon see how important it is to focus on the three crucial aspects of mind, body and soul to become a one-woman revolution, as well as uncover and recognize the super rock star you truly are.

"(As girls,) we don't celebrate enough of our successes. On the soccer field, the basketball court, or even in the classroom, celebrate all your successes no matter how big or small." ~ Mia Hamm

This is your one-woman revolution workbook and inspiration source all in one! The best part about it is... it's all about YOU... so it can't ever be wrong. (How often in life can you say that!?)

"Don't let anyone tell you that you can't do something. Make your own victories. Make your own mistakes." ~ Joan Jett

What are the key elements needed to ROCK out as a one-woman revolution? I'm so glad you asked because they happen to be listed here:

R-Resilience

"You have a dream, and you have obstacles in front of you as we all do. None of us ever get through this life without heartache, without turmoil, and if you believe and you have faith, and you can get knocked down and get back up again, and you believe in perseverance as a great human quality, you find your way." ~ Diana Nyad

A one-woman revolution bounces back and finds opportunity in the things that stress her, challenge her or try to bring her down. (In life or her fitness goals.) She gets up when she falls and comes back even stronger. For a moment, let's consider Elastagirl from the movie *The Incredibles*. She's a Superhero, and her freakin' Superpower is resilience! No matter how often, or in what ways that woman is stressed, strained or stretched to the limit, she bounces back to herself every single time. This is a superpower we can all attain. A one-woman revolution knows that she can't be a victim and victorious at the same time - so we get up after we fall and keep moving forward.

O-Optimism
"You can't live a positive life with a negative mind." ~ Miley Cyrus

Mary Lou Retton once said, "Optimism is a happiness magnet. If you stay positive, good things and good people will be drawn to you." When you're an athlete and one-woman revolution, you focus on the positive, even when things get tough. That's one of the many amazing superpowers you gain from being an athlete. Right now, you may be saying to yourself...'well, I'm not an athlete.' Then maybe you picked up the wrong book! (Kidding!) But seriously, I believe it was Bill Bowerman who said, "if you have a body you are an athlete," and I heartily agree with him. Don't fall into the trap that you have to be a WNBA caliber player, complete 100-mile endurance races, or compete in Ironman Triathlons to consider yourself an athlete.

Being an athlete is a mindset and a way of life that is accessible to everyone. It affects how you respond to adversity; your mental and physical well-being; and the way you set and achieve your goals. A positive outlook is an often overlooked and underutilized superpower to achieve happiness and health. Make no mistake - when the big O comes on strong, it can make the difference between a life of gratitude and joy or bitterness and negativity. (What?! I was referring to Optimism. Get your mind out of the gutter, rockstar!)

<u>C- Courage</u>
"You just have to go full out with confi-
dence and be courageous."
~ Gabby Douglas

An athlete, and a one-woman revolution, isn't afraid to break barriers. They are warriors, and they try new things that they haven't already mastered in order to challenge themselves and grow. Courage takes time to build. Much like building your metaphorical personal house, it doesn't happen - and you don't want it to happen - overnight. As you rock out your adventure of self-discovery, you might find that you want to work on the foundation of your house, redraw some of the blueprints, or start the whole construction project over again. It doesn't matter how many times you need to rebuild. (On the upside, unlike with an actual home, there are no contractors, budgets or time constraints to worry about.)

A one-woman revolution gains confidence and courage by learning from her mistakes - all while understanding and accepting that she can be both scared and courageous at the same time. There is much power to be had when we understand that this is not only possible, but also true.

"You'll never know what you're capable of until you take that first step and just go for it." ~ *Natasha Hastings.*

K-Killing Stereotypes

"You learn that the only way to get rock star power as a girl is to be a groupie and bare your breasts and get chosen for the night. We learn that the only way to get anywhere is through men. And it's a lie."
~ Kathleen Hanna

You can absolutely be an athlete - and superhero - in whatever form that may take for you! A one-woman revolution rebels against labels (unless it's a record label) and refuses to be put in a neat little category or box. Fuck that!

Despite age...what people might think or say...limitations, size, race, creed, sexual preference, color, or otherwise... we can constantly discover and rediscover things about ourselves we never knew, what we're capable of, and take great strides to achieve anything our human heart desires. Every day, we can break negative stereotypes in a positive way. We can change the way the world sees us and even the way we see ourselves in the world.

We can be strong and beautiful - on the inside and the outside - in our own unique ways. Don't be afraid of being too much of anything, being your best self, or of not being the perfect specimen of what someone else thinks you should be. I believe the things that make art and different types of rock music beautiful is that there are so many ways to do it - and that there is beauty in uniqueness as well as imperfection. That's what makes it art and revolutionary (just like you)! So, let's get down and dirty, and ROCK on with our bad selves in the pages that follow.

"My definition of freedom is knowing who you are, and then being it, no matter what anyone else is doing." ~ P!nk

"We're held to a different standard than men. Some guy said to me: 'Don't you think you're too old to sing Rock N' Roll?' I said you'd better check with Mick Jagger." ~ Cher

PART ONE
LAYING THE FOUNDATION

(Resilience)

"It was when I stopped searching for home within others
and lifted the foundations of home within myself that I
found there were no roots more intimate than those between a mind and body that have decided to be whole."
~ Rupi Kaur

We all have the power to be whole, and to make changes in our lives that will make us happier and healthier individuals. It's easy to get overwhelmed, not know where to start and - and as a result - just give up. This is why it's so important to simply start at the beginning- from the ground up, so to speak. In order for something (including us) to be strong and resilient, there has to be a solid foundation. Don't let that scare you off. Building a strong base is easier to do than you're giving yourself credit for. (Yes, I read your mind.) For example, I find that I'm able to compete in endurance events now, with a lot less training and running mileage, because I have an incredible fitness base to work from. This means that over the past 20ish years as an endurance athlete, three crucial elements have allowed me to build up my fitness levels and sustain them with less time and effort now than I needed when I first started. These three key elements are priorities, consistency and resilience. Without making myself and my fitness goals a priority, remaining consistent with my training over the years, and not letting adversity or obstacles keep me down, I wouldn't have such a killer base to work from.

"A journey of a thousand miles begins with a single step."
~ Lao Tzu

We need to start with a good foundation, but as humans, we like to get ahead of ourselves. Maybe we're comparing ourselves as a beginner of something to someone who has been doing that particular thing for many years. We get discouraged and quit before we even get started. Everything needs a foundation for it to not only work well but for it to last.

As an organization, Girls with Sole kicks ass and works well because it's based on the foundation of utilizing mind, body and soul to ROCK. Girls with Sole programs provide the girls with the tools to move forward with resilience, make physical and mental health a priority, and to Lace Up for a Lifetime of Achievement!

The programs give the girls a chance to break out of their comfort zones, tap into an inner source of strength, and clear space in their minds to reach their true potential and inner superheroes. The seeds are planted, begin to take root and create their base. From there, they can rely on this newfound Resilience, Optimism and Courage to begin Killing Stereotypes - and then share it all with others by creating a ripple effect of their powers.

Rock music is no different. It had to start somewhere, and without a strong foundation, it would have never lasted this long or been so incredibly impactful to so many people around the world. No matter what genre of music you listen to today, it has stemmed from Rock & Roll. Without Rock coming in and literally shaking things up in a fresh, exciting and different way, the foundation for pop, R&B, Rap, Punk, Alternative and others would be nonexistent. The loud voice of the singer, along with the amplified guitar, and heavy drums and bass produced an energy and passion that influenced people's perceptions of both music and entertainment, creating a long-lasting base for all genres to build upon in their own unique and awesome ways. If you've made it this far in the book - you're on a mission!

So, let's create a personal mission statement since it's vital to our base or foundation to rock the house.

"I will not be a rock star. I will be a legend."
- Freddie Mercury

Girls with Sole Mission Statement: "Use fitness and wellness to empower the minds, bodies and souls of girls who have experienced abuse of any kind, or who are at-risk." A mission statement explains who you are and who you want to be. It shows the world what you are about.

Write your personal mission statement here. Keep in mind that a mission statement is a lot like your personal house. It can be rethought, revised and reconstructed as many times as you need to. It's all about you: your values, beliefs, how you see yourself, what you want to achieve, and how you will (consistently) do it - so don't be afraid to rock that shit out.

Awesome! You have created a kickass mission statement that will set the tone for your base! This is pretty exciting shit - your foundation is already looking solid - but there's more work to do, so don't drop the mic quite yet.

"Your beliefs become your thoughts,
Your thoughts become your words,
Your words become your actions,
Your actions become your habits,
Your habits become your values,
Your values become your destiny."
~Gandhi

It's impossible to lay a foundation for change or improvement without reflecting on our beliefs, values, and what already resides in our hearts. While creating the foundation of our "house" is crucial, so too is the actual place we choose to build upon. A one-woman revolution wouldn't choose to build her house on property that didn't belong to her or on swamp land that couldn't support it.

Since our beliefs govern our lives, and can either limit or empower us, it's extremely important to know what they are and if they are truly our own, or too heavily influenced by others.

Let's explore some core beliefs by listing what each of the following words mean to you. Try not to overthink it. Go with your initial thoughts and feelings when you read each word and list their meaning to you in the space provided. Be brutally honest.

Fitness

Change

Family

Success

Forgiveness

Failure_____	Control_____
_____	_____
_____	_____
Loyalty_____	Faith_____
_____	_____
_____	_____
Sex_____	Money_____
_____	_____
_____	_____
Freedom_____	Politics_____
_____	_____
_____	_____
Love_____	Life_____
_____	_____
_____	_____
Women_____	Men_____
_____	_____
_____	_____

Look at the beliefs you have listed above and consider the ones that may not feel like your own because they were influenced by how you were raised, or by friends or loved ones. Do any of the beliefs listed above make you feel uneasy or conflicted? If they do, it's never too late to adjust them and make them your own, in order to be strengthened, as opposed to, hindered by them. Since life isn't a spectator sport, you need to fully participate in choosing your own reality. To truly believe what you believe and the values that govern your life. Do you want to see the good? See it. This might be the point in time when you want to sit back and say- well, it's not that simple. Well, to that I call bullshit, because as ridiculous as this might sound, it kinda is that simple. Are you angry instead of at peace? Are you resentful instead of grateful? It's little changes in your beliefs and perceptions that can change your entire life.

You already have everything you need to build your foundation inside of you. You just have to dig deep. I know firsthand that exploring, and possibly changing, your beliefs justifiably takes time and can be a daunting or scary prospect. Be patient and kind to yourself during the process. Dare I say, have fun on the adventure?

If you begin to feel overwhelmed, consider the following story from one of my running adventures. In May of 2017, I had the chance to run the Great Wall Marathon in China, widely acknowledged to be one of the toughest races in the world. I had an awesome conversation with a fellow runner on the actual Great Wall itself. She told me that when things get tough, she asks herself: "What can I do in the next five minutes to make my situation better?" Breaking down what seems to be overwhelmingly painful or emotionally daunting into 5-minute increments and creating solutions to improve just the next five minutes is surprisingly impactful. Improving our situation, even for a short amount a time, can make everything seem easier to handle and resilience even more possible - and in turn, creates a rock-solid foundation.

What can you focus on for 5 minutes that would improve how you think and feel right now? Maybe, it's telling the author to "fuck off" and getting a good laugh out of it. I'm okay with that if it helps you.

"Although we may have many positive influences around us, only we can control our own destinies. The only limitations are those you put on yourself." ~ Lisa Fernandez

Now that we've explored our core beliefs, it's time to peek at fostering our self-awareness. What is self-awareness? I know self-help gurus have different names and definitions for self-awareness, but to me, being self-aware means having the ability to look within ourselves in order to gain a clear picture of our emotions, motivations and our personality in general. It's about truly understanding ourselves so that we can move forward in life, relationships and fitness, and gain resilience to reach goals and make positive changes when we feel it's needed. With improved self-awareness, we can understand our thoughts and emotions more easily and figure out what our true motivations are. Self-awareness is important because once we can figure these things out about ourselves, we can make the changes we need to be resilient, to grow as a person and to make our life better.

Consider the following questions and write your answers in the space provided.

What makes me unique?

_____

_____

_____

_____

What am I passionate about?

_____

_____

_____

_____

What does 'healthy' mean to me?

_____

_____

_____

_____

What are my best and worst qualities?

_____

_____

_____

What am I most proud of?

_____

_____

_____

_____

What do I fear?

_____

_____

_____

_____

How do I overcome obstacles?

_____

_____

_____

_____

What are my goals for the next few months (personal, professional and fitness)?

_____

_____

_____

_____

If you had to draw a life map from right now - with the destination being 5 years from now - what would that look like? (Sorry, you can't use Google Maps for this one!) Draw your map below:

"It's like if you plant something in the concrete and if it grows and the rose petal got all kinds of scratches and marks, you ain't gonna say, 'Damn, look at all the scratches and marks on the rose that grew from the concrete.' You're gonna be like, 'Damn, a rose grew from the concrete?'" ~ *Tupac Shakur*

The final section in Part One zones in on resilience itself, because it's the cement that holds everything together and creates the durability for our foundation to lift our house, carry the weight and withstand any storms that try to shake it.

I can't stress enough how important resiliency is to the strength of our foundation. Like the character Elastagirl from the movie *The Incredibles*, I like to think of resilience as my superpower as well. Believe me; I'm a true empath. I feel everything, and I let these feelings rip me apart every night, but my Superpower keeps me from dying. Instead, I grow more open and make more room for strength in my life to overcome and keep moving forward.

I feel an actual lump in my throat of sadness when I think of how many people could have a completely different, happier, more fulfilling life if they only realized how resilient they could be.

"You can't stop the waves, but you can learn to surf."
~ *Jon Kabat-Zinn*

With social media as prevalent as it is - we're constantly seeing split-second snapshots into people's lives that lead us to believe they are glamorous, perfect, exciting and always happy. If we lack resilience, we may fall more easily into a victimized mindset when things go wrong. It would be easer to look at those snapshots today and think or say things such as "I hate my life," "Things are just easier for other people"; "Why do bad things always happen to me?"; "That person has nothing to worry about"; or

"Other people don't have to deal with the same things that I do."

Perhaps people have thought these things while looking at me - both now and when I was younger - yet, during my life (then and now) I have personally dealt - or still deal with - foster care, sexual abuse, domestic violence, PTSD, depression, anxiety, substance abuse in my family and the death of my ex-husband after a long battle with alcoholism - among other things.

Traumatic experiences happen to everyone: truly, no one is immune. Believe me, I understand that it's tempting to give up after something blows up in your face and shakes the foundation you worked so hard to establish. **What's the alternative to being resilient? I believe the only alternative is living your life as a victim, feeling bitter, sad, and not wanting to try anything new** or take risks. Without resilience, it's all too easy to live a shuttered and unfulfilling

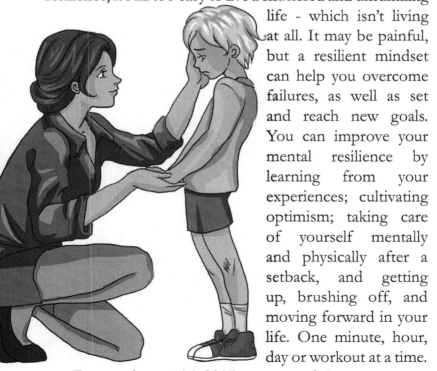

life - which isn't living at all. It may be painful, but a resilient mindset can help you overcome failures, as well as set and reach new goals. You can improve your mental resilience by learning from your experiences; cultivating optimism; taking care of yourself mentally and physically after a setback, and getting up, brushing off, and moving forward in your life. One minute, hour, day or workout at a time.

For me, August 16, 2015, was one of those unexpected, difficult days that literally shook me in mind, body and soul, and tested my inner strength and resilience. It was the day that I ran the Leading Ladies Marathon in Spearfish, South Dakota, and it was the day that my ex-husband, Joe, (the biological father of my son, Jake) died.

The night before, I tossed and turned in my hotel bed; kept awake by a mix of pre-race jitters infused with anxiety that had been with me for weeks. I experienced an irrational and unexplainable fear that something terrible was about to happen. I didn't have any idea what it was that might happen, but I was so afraid (and felt in my soul) that whatever it was - was going to happen to Jake. I suppose my premonition was right. Joe died in his sleep due to heart failure. There was so much damage to his body from years of binge drinking and smoking, the coroner said that although he was only 45-years-old, his heart was that of a 95-year-old man. Even though I had unexplained anxiety leading into this trip, I was so excited about it because I had planned it together with an old friend from high school, named Fiona, who grew up in Rochester, New York but now lives in Custer, South Dakota with her amazing family and beautiful animals of every kind! She and I were on the track team together in high school, and although I hadn't seen her in a very long time, we reconnected on Facebook, where she learned of my quest of running a marathon in all 50 states for Girls with Sole. There were many times that I felt as if my 50 States For Sole campaign took on a life of it's own, and along with the help of the Universe, it made sure I was always where I needed to be - exactly when I needed to be there.

Fiona reached out to me on Facebook to tell me about the Leading Ladies Marathon, and just like that - my South Dakota marathon had been chosen. I would run the full marathon while Fiona ran the half marathon - and the best part would be reuniting with an old friend, staying at her house and meeting her family.

I stepped off the plane in the toy-sized Custer Airport and made my way to the tiny gate area where Fiona was waiting for me with two of her four children. The kids were the only evidence that more than 25 years had passed, since Fiona looked exactly the same as I remembered her in high school. A heart-warming sense of pride and gratefulness in regard to 50 States For Sole accompanied my happiness and excitement, for, without it, I most likely wouldn't have made the trip out to see her in Custer, South Dakota - and I was so glad I did.

Fiona is a documentary filmmaker and television producer for PBS, so she's not only hilarious, intelligent, beautiful, athletic and the most wonderful friend and mom, but this woman is also a storyteller at heart. After saying our hellos and giving out hugs, instead of leaving the gate area, we waited around to see how various other stories played out as passengers disembarked from the plane and were greeted by family members, girlfriends and spouses. It was hilarious. Fiona knew what each person's story was and whom they were waiting to greet. She had a special soft spot for the young bride waiting to be reunited with her soldier-husband. Thus, we waited to see it all unfold so that Fiona could feed her soul with another beautiful story.

When we finally departed the airport and drove to Fiona's home, I discovered Fiona actually resides in heaven on earth. She lives on a ranch with horses, cows (she said one of the cows was an asshole - so he was chosen to be eaten first), chickens, kittens, and the biggest, goofiest, most awesomely beautiful St. Bernard that you have ever seen since that old movie, Beethoven. Oh yeah- and her wonderful husband and children were there too! I can't even describe what a truly beautiful family and life they have all created.

That night, we went to a party at her friend's house, which was an amazing wonderland of a place as well.

A giant movie screen played music videos to entertain the kids, and there was a playhouse in the yard for them that I believe may have been bigger and nicer than my actual home. I loved it! Everyone was so kind, giving and welcoming, and her friend's home was like a magical place, decorated in a way that made you feel like you had stepped into a storybook. The decor was part Alice in Wonderland, and part elegant dude ranch resort, mixed with just the right amount of an Anthropologie vibe to make me feel like I had stepped onto my Mother Ship. There were a few little boys in the most adorable cowboy hats and boots so small you would think they were made for stuffed animals instead of humans. Fiona had to remind me that the kids were from rancher families and although adorable, they weren't wearing costumes. The next day, the whole family hung out with me, showing me the awe-inspiring Black Hills, the "famous" penis shaped mountain, and the slightly more famous, Mt. Rushmore. The plan for later in that day was for Fiona and I to go to a hotel located closer to the Lead Country Club race start, since the darn thing would go off at 6:00 am, and Fiona's home was roughly an hour away. We intended to stay in the hotel the night before the race, run, and then return to Fiona's house to continue with more sightseeing, which would include a visit to the Crazy Horse Memorial. We all know that the best intentions and best-laid plans can change in an instant - but we never know just when that instant will be. At the ass-crack of dawn, Fiona and I said our good-byes and good lucks as she and I were running in two different races with different start times.

I started my 26.2 journey just after sunrise, and ran the first few miles on a gorgeous dirt road, surrounded by intense natural beauty. I had never taken part in an all-female race, which made this beautiful course even more special to me.

Running through Spearfish Canyon with towering cliffs and alongside the creek was breathtaking. We ran out of Lead and along the Scenic Byway of Spearfish Canyon where you can actually feel the pulse of the West come alive in Deadwood, and John Dunbar befriended the Sioux Indians as he danced with wolves.

I'm not going to lie - my legs and body didn't feel as beautiful as my surroundings looked. The elevation was sort of kicking my ass, and I was glad to hear from my fellow runners that I wasn't the only one it was affecting. It's good to be reminded that we're all running the same course, in the same conditions, and that you aren't the only one feeling the effects of the non-discriminatory pain. As I ran alongside and chatted with some incredible women, I was once again struck by yet another "sign" that I was doing exactly what was meant to be done for Girls with Sole. Of all the people I could have been running next to, and commiserating with, it's no accident that Missy Woodruff- a teacher from my hometown of Rochester, New York, was the one. We were a thousand miles away from home, with hundreds of women running in the race, and I just "happened" to run up to someone from where I grew up and proceeded to dazzle her with a crazy one-liner about bacon and body oder. I turned to her and made the declaration that I smelled bacon. I asked if she did as well, but she said she didn't, so I said that it must have been my B.O. that I was smelling. If that isn't a sure sign that my mission is working, I don't know what is. Either she was too tired to run away from me, or she was intrigued. Recently, during some communication we had via Facebook Messenger, she told me it was the latter.

We ran together for many difficult miles, both of us feeling that special brand of discomfort that comes with running 26.2 miles in a canyon when you aren't used to an elevation of any kind. Of course, she and I discussed Girls with Sole, and of course, my heart overflowed when she reached out to me after the race on Facebook, hoping to one day bring much-needed Girls with Sole programming to her school.

At the finish line, I was shocked to discover that I had finished 3rd in my 45-49 age group, because I don't usually place in the marathons I run, and I felt relieved and thrilled to see my overjoyed friend, Fiona, cheering for me.

We drove back to the hotel to grab a shower before heading back to her house. I felt ill from either the altitude, mileage, dehydration or all of the above - and threw up in the bathroom before getting in the shower. I usually check my phone and call my family directly after finishing a marathon, but I needed to collect myself and try to feel better before I picked up the phone.

Fiona and I got ready to head back to her house, and after I threw up once or twice again, we got in her car, and I checked my phone. There were emergency texts from my husband in all capital letters to call him. He let me know that the kids were fine, but I needed to call ASAP. Because my mom was almost 90 years old at the time, my thoughts shot immediately to her and that she had died.

I called Frank and was completely floored to hear that it was, in fact, Joe who had passed away. My heart sank into my stomach, and I felt flooded with so much emotion and sadness for my son, Jake, and deep concern for how this would affect him, as well, as my daughter, Morgan. Suddenly, I may have well been sitting on Mars or some other distant planet, instead of in a hotel parking lot in South Dakota because I felt light years away from my children who I wanted to see and hold at that moment more than anything in the world.

Being there with my friend, who has a heart bigger than the Black Hills themselves, was so meant to be. She drove me straight to the airport while my husband changed my flights to get me home. Zombie-like, I made my way to the gate, sat down on the floor next to it, and sobbed. Understandably, people stared. I had just purchased a Coke Zero which, immediately upon sitting down, I accidentally knocked over and spilled all over the floor. I sat there in a heap, and instead of cleaning it up, I just let my tears pool and spill over into the puddle of it on the carpet. An extremely kind and concerned janitor came over to see if I was okay. She kneeled beside me, mopped up the spilled soda, and with the kindness of a mother to a child, said that it's often helpful to talk to people we don't know when things are bothering us. In between canyon-sized sobs, I told her I didn't want to talk about it. She understood, but also notified security, who then also came over to see if I was okay. I'm pretty sure they were quite concerned about my sanity and the chance that I might do something crazy either in the airport or on the flight. I tried really hard to pull myself together but was utterly consumed with worry about Jake, and Morgan too. How would this affect all of us individually and as a family? I knew that Joe would die young and that this day was inevitable - but even so, it came as a painful shock. The damage to his body from years of alcoholism and smoking cigarettes was extensive and irreversible. Another thing that is irreversible is the great pain associated with guilt, and I thank God and the Universe for the fact that none of us have to bear that kind of hurt in our hearts. Joe had been sober for the last two years of his life, and although he wasn't around for the daily duties or financial obligations of parenthood, he made great efforts in seeing Jake for an occasional breakfast and attended his swimming and track meets with great pride. He maintained a residence and a good job at the end of his life, and although he didn't have any family to speak of, he was a part of ours. On holidays and other occasions, Joe joined our family - not just because he was Jake's biological dad, but also because we didn't want him to be alone. We never robbed him of spending time with Jake when he was sober. Jake was the one thing in Joe's life that he was genuinely proud of - and the only thing that made him feel like he'd done something right in his life. Jake was everything to him; his world. There was a great portion of Jake's life that Joe missed due to his drinking, but I'm grateful that at the end he was doing well and was as involved with Jake as could be expected. We would never have to feel bad about that, which I feel we all found immensely comforting.

About a week before Joe passed away, he asked Jake to go on an overnight camping trip with him. This was something that had been discussed in the past but had never come to fruition in all of Jake's 17 years. At first, there was some reservation about doing an overnight trip with Joe, but Jake decided that he would go, and ended up having a really nice time. We didn't know it at the time, but Jake's decision to spend time with Joe in a tent in the woods ended up being a profoundly impactful decision; one that I know we're all glad about.

Joe's life decisions may have haunted him, but they didn't have to haunt us because we can focus on the positive times we had with him at the end, and the fact that Jake and Morgan both have the most amazing father in the world in Frank.

Frank has been the only father figure Jake has known, and has been in Jake's life since he was twelve months old. He has provided a strong foundation of love, stability and guidance to both Jake and Morgan. Because Frank is a kind, strong and compassionate man - he was even a father figure of sorts to Joe as well. Joe often came to him for advice, for help, and sometimes to borrow money, and Frank always gave him what he needed. He was respectful to Joe, and Joe held Frank in high regard, and I believe, he was grateful in his own way that Jake had Frank in his life to provide what he couldn't: simultaneously filling and breaking his heart.

During my life, I had made many mistakes and fallen many times. Perhaps going to Vegas and marrying Joe two and half weeks after meeting him was looked upon by some people as one of my many mistakes, but I will never see it that way. While it was often difficult, my impulsive decision to marry Joe resulted in the most amazing gift that is Jake. I bided my time until I was ready to meet Frank and create the strongest knit and beautiful family I could have ever dreamed of.

Frank, Jake and Morgan are the most remarkable human beings. As an adopted child, with no knowledge of anyone I'm blood related to, I'm proud to have created a family and a foundation built upon their love and my own resilience. At one period of my life, I believed I would never have or deserved any of these things, which is one of the many reasons why I treasure them so much. It will take some effort, but I know I can eventually let go of the fear and worry for my children that tries to cast a long, dark shadow over a corner of my heart.

They will continue to move forward and bring light to the world no matter what happens, because we have each other, and our pasts will never determine our future. This story brings us back to the utmost importance of resilience once again. Am I beating a poor, dead horse? I don't think I am. I truly believe resilience is this vital to us all.

So, how do we, as humans, take on resilience as a superpower? My first response is always to build physical strength and endurance. In whatever way you can. Running, swimming, lifting, boxing, dancing, yoga, cycling... find your way to challenge yourself physically and the mental strength will follow. How we view adversity and stress strongly affects how we succeed, and this is one of the most important reasons that having a resilient mindset is so important.

Being physically and mentally fit, and pushing ourselves past our comfort zones helps us to develop all the necessary attributes of a resilient person. Consider this: like an athlete, a resilient person actively maintains an optimistic outlook and actually sees their life as good, even if their current or past situations were not ideal. They believe good things will happen to them in the future, even during the toughest times.

A resilient person works hard at staying true to themselves, to their beliefs, values and their goals, and does their best to not let other people's opinions or drama drag them down. Instead, they focus their time and energy on changing the things that they can control and never play the role of victim when things don't go well for them, or they experience hardships.

Honestly, I wouldn't be here today without the resilience I built by being fit and fierce in mind, body and soul. My priorities revolve around my happiness and my sanity - and believing in myself and my abilities - all of which are derived from running and fitness. Without this rock-solid foundation, I couldn't take a single step forward in building the rest of my house. When I finally figured that out and consistently built my resilience brick by brick, I was able to live contently in a house that sole built. The storms and hurricanes still come, and they still rattle me, but fuck that- I rock!

Yes, I spelled sole like that on purpose. Running may not be everyone's favorite thing, but I will always sing the praises of what running can do for your mental health, inner strength and the ability to conquer any negative shit life tries to chuck at your head.

It's okay if you don't feel entirely confident taking advice about resilience, how to cultivate it, and how it is directly correlated to fitness from a goofball like me. (Frankly, I don't blame you)

Gretchen Reynolds has been writing about running and fitness for more than a decade. As the Phys Ed columnist for *The New York Times*, she gets to geek out and report on the work of physiologists, exercise scientists, and experts in a broad range of scientific disciplines. As a fan of her work, I was thrilled to talk with her about everything she's learned about fitness.

One of the more surprising things I learned from Gretchen is a psychological term called "self-efficacy"— the realization that you are more capable than you think you are. She told me that people who begin moving more, especially those that start running, test higher on scales that measure self-efficacy, not only in terms of exercise but basically everywhere else as well. It's been proven over and over again in sports science that running can change lives. Gretchen told me, "That's one of the reasons I love running, love writing about running, and one of the reasons that I think running is really important and has the capability to change lives." She said, "I know that sounds like a cliché, but it does appear to consistently be true."

For Gretchen, running has taught her how to rock with resilience. "I am not a particularly powerful runner, but I will keep doing it because it helps me when times are tough. One year, my father, my husband, and my son all became pretty ill, and it was really stressful. I was able to cope better when I went out and ran. I was able to come back with a clear head and deal with whatever needed to be dealt with."

Through her work reporting on the latest research, Gretchen told me that she has learned why running makes us resilient and is so good for us. "There are not a lot of downsides [to running], from a physiological perspective. It's one of the few, as they say in drug research trials, interventions with nearly all upside. And, yes you can get injured, and almost everybody does at some point, but those are pretty minor injuries. Almost everyone who starts [running] will find that even if it's not pleasant at first… the body adjusts, and it starts becoming easier, and you start feeling more powerful. Even once you run a marathon, you can still improve, and I don't just mean becoming faster—you can still find a certain magic in running that I'm not sure you get from any other activity.

"One of the most surprising things I've learned working for *The New York Times*—and it still gets attention every time I write about it—is the idea that our brains are not static. When I was a student taking biology, we were taught that we all get a certain number of brain cells and that's it—you killed them off for the rest of your life, but that's not true. Our brains are plastic, and we can make more neurons all the time. Being fit, and in particular becoming fit by running, can *quadruple* the number of new brain cells that you make. That changes your brain more effectively than anything else you do in your life." To me, that's a holy-shit conclusion because it means that exercise is not just a matter of staying fit, but can actually be a way to make your body biologically resilient. We can keep our brain, the most fundamental organ in our bodies, healthy and functioning well throughout our lives. And science has shown that the best way to do that, pretty clearly, is by running.

I would never - by any stretch of the imagination - consider myself a scientist, and I have often joked that Girls with Sole isn't exactly "rocket science," but I have to agree with Gretchen, and love having science back up what I have known (from experience) to be true for my entire life.

Being able to bounce back when obstacles get in your way, and life pulls you down, is the key to living an empowered and happy life. Many people might say they agree with this line of thinking, but often people don't practice what they preach. Running can help fix that real quick. For me, running marathons can mirror life in many ways — as they both present their own set of obstacles and adversity to potentially "derail" us on our journey.

Little did I know that while running a marathon in Indiana during my 50 States For Sole campaign, I would come face to face with the literal version of this life lesson!

If I could stress any one thing about running a marathon in all 50 states, it's that - much like life - obstacles are all part of the adventure. During the 50 States for Sole journey, I came up against some tough ones, including altitude sickness; a ruptured cyst on my ovary at mile 18 of a marathon course; a fatal shooting on a highway we were traveling on to get to a race that closed it down for hours; a car driving towards us head-on at 80 miles per hour on the wrong side of the road on the way to a race; storms; broken down vehicles; and other various adventures involving my travel, accommodations, or the marathons themselves, to name a few.

One marathon, in particular, stands out in my mind as a literal lesson in resilience and the fact that although we can't control everything, we can control how we react and how it can affect our mind, body and soul.

I started the 26.2 mile run in the very quaint town of Columbus, Indiana, and as I ran, I took in the scenery with a wonderful sense of satisfaction that I was on the right track. My purpose in life is to help empower girls in need through the Girls with Sole programming, and to raise my own children – whom I carry in my heart at every race and on every trip I take. While I ran the Mill Race Marathon, I thought about how fortunate I am to have a family at home who loves me and supports me in my efforts to change the lives of girls who need Girls with Sole in order to be as strong and happy in their lives as I am today.

At about mile two or three, a physical reminder of what GWS is about, and why I am doing what I'm doing was placed in front of me – quite literally – in the form of a freight train! I looked up and saw that there was a commotion as runners approached the tracks. Most of the runners veered off to take an alternative route, while others ran up to the train and stopped as close to the tracks as they could get. When I got close enough to decide which way I wanted to go, I decided to wait at the tracks. Again – much like life – I decided that following the crowd would not be in my best interest. Since I wasn't familiar with the area, I had no idea how far out of the way the other route might take me – or how much of the course may have been cut off if I followed the people who ran off across the grassy field to who knows where.

As I reached the crowd of astonished runners gathered

in front of the slowly moving train, it begrudgingly came to a halt, and I heard a man behind me yell angrily (twice) "THIS IS BULLSHIT!"

I was just as shocked as everyone else by this crazy situation. I have been an endurance athlete for over 20 years and have completed hundreds of races – but this is the first time I have ever been stopped on a race course by a train!

They say nothing can stop a train – and that might be true – but nothing can stop a runner either! And that's a fact!

Some of the runners actually started to climb through the cars and jump over the railroad tracks to keep moving forward on the course. Although the train was moving slowly, climbing through the cars seemed a ludicrous and highly dangerous option in my opinion.

The guy behind me paced and huffed, and I couldn't help but stand there and smile.

This is all part of the experience – the journey. We can try to control everything with our training plans, race plans, and Garmins, but it's impossible to do so. Shit is gonna happen anyway, and we have to find a way to deal with it and move forward. Yes, my time was going to be about three to five minutes slower, but in the big scheme of things, so what? I knew that I would need to stop to pee at least once while I was out there – which would also slow my time down. Most of the time, for me, doing a race is about being there and experiencing everything possible, and then using those experiences to strengthen and empower myself and others, as well as to enrich my own life while leaving a legacy for my kids and the girls in my programs. And, not to be a jerk, but anyone who was running the same pace as me at that particular race, wasn't going to win or qualify for Boston anyway.

At any time in our lives, we can be moving along on the right track, and the wrong train can come along, derailing our stride. The important thing is to work through it –

and to make the choice to stay positive and keep moving forward!! I saw a really cool quote recently that I shared with my husband, my daughter and son because I think it's something so important for everyone to remember. It said: "Emotions are like waves. You can't stop them from coming – but you can choose which ones to surf."

The train finally pulled away, making room for the runners to get by and continue on our way. I listened to various miffed conversations about finishing times and pace being thrown off. I told one of the ladies running next to me that I was just glad to be there, completing another state. She looked at me like I was the village idiot who had escaped again and was running loose. I didn't care. She has her journey, and I have mine.

My journey isn't the same as anyone else's, and I love and embrace that fact. Sometimes, when things like this happen, I am reminded that bigger obstacles have tried to stop me in my life, but they couldn't. Compared to those things, a train ain't shit. The heart and soul of a survivor are stronger than any obstacle when our energy finds the right focus. A Girl With Sole finds the focus that turns negative energy into a positive force – and that's a runaway train that can't be stopped.

Aside from the train holding things up a bit, everything else about this marathon was on the right track! All the details about this little race could easily rival the big-time race venues that I have experienced. The Expo was fantastic, and so were the race shirts, bibs, medals and support on the course – both from spectators and volunteers. They did an amazing job organizing, and the whole town seemed to support the runners and embrace the race itself. Each of the mile markers had unique and creative artwork made by local school children, which was a touch I really loved.

At the start of the race, it was about 53 degrees. There was a great DJ and a short opening ceremony which included the singing of "The Star-Spangled Banner" by two local high school girls. The day got pretty hot with temps reaching the mid-80s, but the course offered some great architecture, scenery, and wonderful energy from the crowd. Many marathon runners don't agree with me, but I tend to enjoy the small, college town races more than the super-crowded, huge city ones.

I just loved the small-town charm combined with the professional feel of a big-time race! For me, that's a winning combination. The icing on the cake was having a message (in the form of a train) park itself in front of me as I worked towards completing my journey of 50 States for Sole. The message reminded me not only of my own strength and resilience, but also the gratitude I have for my health, my family and my life....and that Girls with Sole is truly on the right track to bringing these same realizations to girls everywhere.

We all have the power, and the choice, to ROCK.

PART TWO
CREATING YOUR DESIGN

(Optimism)

"No matter who you are, no matter what you did, no matter where you've come from, you can always change, become a better version of yourself." ~ Madonna

Often, people ask me how I do some of the things I do. For example, when I ran a marathon on the Great Wall of China that included over 5,000 vertical steps, or when I did one in all 50 States in 2.5 years (sometimes on back-to-back days), it blew me away how many people would ask, "How did you do that?" The question actually stumped me every time because being the self-explainer and people-pleaser that I am; I wanted to give an elaborate answer. An answer that would give the person enough information to feel that I wasn't being boastful, that they too could achieve these things (which they could) with elaborate planning and extensive soul-searching, because that's what I thought they wanted to hear. But then I remembered, 'Fuck that - I rock!' and told them the absolute, real, basic and raw answer (which holds true for the way I have approached all of my achievements in life) which is: I just did it.

Saying, 'I just did it' isn't cocky or sarcastic - it's the foundation and base for starting any huge endeavor, approaching a new goal, or changing your life for the better. So, it sounds like I'm being an asshole when really I've learned to train myself to approach and achieve my goals, or what I want out of life, with the right mindset. Instead of getting caught up in all the reasons I might not be able to do something like the old Nike slogan said, I just do it. Our thoughts are so powerful, that without a courageous and positive mindset, we can very easily talk ourselves out of attempting to make changes or go after the things we want to achieve. What we choose to believe about ourselves becomes true for us, so my approach to life mirrors the beginning of Rob Zombie's song, *Thunder Kiss '65*, which is a line sampled from the 1965 movie, *Faster Pussycat! Kill! Kill!* The line is delivered by a kickass female actress, and she quips: "I never try anything; I just do it. Wanna try me?" Or as Yoda once said, "do or do not. There is no try."

Okay, so how the hell do you get a positive mindset, anyway? I'm not a mindset magician, but I do have a few tricks up my sleeve that have worked for me - so they can most definitely work for you. One of these tricks is exercise and fitness.

It doesn't matter if it's a walk, swim, bike ride, run, yoga or whatever it is that moves your body and makes your soul sing - exercise can turn negative thoughts into positive ones and bad attitudes into good ones. Problems don't magically disappear, but after a workout, they are somehow, wondrously so much easier to deal with. It's a way to change our brain chemistry in a natural and healthy way, and tap into a peaceful, powerful and positive place all at once. I have found that physical fitness in any form is a superpower that can conquer depression, anxiety and stress. It turns my negative emotions into energy and my sweat into a magical soul cleanser.

Exercise and fitness lay the foundation for a positive mindset and an optimistic outlook because it serves as an opportunity to focus and breathe; to tune out negativity and to expand your mind with incredible amounts of strength, purpose, power and pride. As an added bonus, it just feels amazing to move, and that's just what our bodies were made to do. There's no better work of art than yourself, and no better way to develop a positive mindset than continuously creating the masterpiece that is you.

"Just don't give up trying to do what you really want to do. Where there is love and inspiration, I don't think you can go wrong."
~ Ella Fitzgerald

When I registered to do it, I suppose I should have been slightly more wary of the fact that the tagline for the Utah Valley Marathon (the one that is proudly and prominently highlighted on everything from their website to the race shirts) is "Pain You Enjoy." But I don't let that stuff get into my head and bother me.

Heck, everyone and their Tough Mudder boasts that their race is the toughest, the meanest, and the most bad-ass on the planet. I have done them all -everything from Dances With Dirt in Hell - with race shirts that actually sport the part of the waiver that warns participants of death as a viable possibility due to the difficulty of the race course - to the Tough Mudder - as well as Ironman and a host of others. They are all tough. They all offer their own laundry list of challenges, but the Utah Valley Marathon had its own special brand of pain- veiled in beauty and breathtaking surroundings.

In a way, the race was much like "Jokey Smurf" from the old *Smurfs* cartoon I used to watch on Saturday mornings as a kid. Jokey would give various other Smurfs a beautifully wrapped present - complete with a big red bow - which, upon opening, would promptly explode in their face. He would laugh and laugh, and they would just stand there, dumbstruck, with black soot and an unhappy look on their face.

As a kid, I always wondered why the Smurfs continued to accept Jokey's presents. The village was pretty small, and they had all been tricked by the exploding gift numerous times, yet they were still drawn in by the big, beautiful box wrapped perfectly with a big, red bow. How on Earth could they be tricked over and over by the same gag?!

Perhaps, as a Captain Crunch scoffing ten-year-old, the subtle innuendo that seemed to escape me as I munched down on a mouth full of crunch berries was that maybe this was pain they enjoyed! They couldn't help themselves. How bad could it really be? Everyone loves a gift, don't they? Wouldn't a little pain for the thrill of the gift be worth it?

Now that I think about it, I bet the Smurfs knew exactly what would happen if they took the gift from Jokey, but they did it anyway, because of the hypnotic excitement of possibility. Possibility holds so much promise, and makes the risk of a little pain worth it, when there is the slightest chance for phenomenal and unique treasures to be found. I suppose that's why we all continue to look for love even after heartbreak - and why I continue to register for races that I know are going to hurt.

The Utah Valley Marathon, voted one of Runner's World Magazine's Top Ten Marathons, is a gift of beauty, wrapped in amazing scenery and feelings of adventure, and the big, red ribbon of promise that the course is all "downhill." Then you open it, and the 3:00 am bus ride up the canyon, elevation, and all the wind and dry air blow up in your face.

At first you stand there a bit stunned by the explosion, but because it's pain you enjoy (crazy Smurf that you are), you would do it again and again since the experience of it all is just that amazing.

That being said, don't think for a minute that I actually enjoy pain. Quite the contrary; I'm the biggest wimp there is. I can hardly stand the sight of a needle, and having a fever can reduce me to tears.

But to me, "Pain You Enjoy" doesn't mean you love pain, necessarily. To me, it means what Girls with Sole and running means to me. To be resilient, we must learn to face our fears and move forward no matter what. If we want to achieve our dreams and our goals, discomfort is a necessity. We can get through it to reach the greater good, and the pain we experience actually makes us stronger and prepares our minds, bodies and souls for the next trying experience that challenges us along the way. We endure because we enjoy the satisfaction of enduring. We love the achievement of breaking through a barrier to prove to ourselves that we could do something we once thought we could never do. We feel uncomfortable at times, but we know that we are Lacing Up for a Lifetime of Achievement.

The Utah Valley Marathon was one that proved to be more than just a little challenging, and was quite honestly, very painful for me at times, but that made the Finish Line Feeling all the sweeter with a sense of achievement as big as the mountains surrounding it.

For a non-morning person, one of the greatest challenges of all could very well have been the fact that we had to catch the bus that took us up into the Canyon for the race start at 3:30 am! The busses started picking up the runners in front of the host hotel at 3:00 am, and they ran continuously until 4:15 am. Taking the last bus was strongly discouraged, of course, since they didn't want every runner trying to get a few extra winks and then all showing up for the same ride. I decided to show up somewhere in the middle and rode the 3:30 bus. The bus filled up quickly with tired, but chatty, nervous runners, and wound through the steep and dark canyon roads until it reached a ranch that had a fenced in pasture devoid of four-legged livestock. Instead, you could look into the pasture and see small groups of humans huddled around short metal drums containing bonfires in the pitch dark. It was pretty cold up there at the elevation of 6,300 feet, and the moon wasn't exactly casting much heat. (Did I also mention that, although I live in Cleveland, Ohio, I absolutely hate to be cold?) Runners of all ages and skill levels sat hunched over as close as possible to the fire without getting burned, or breathing in too much of the smoke that permeated the air. It was incredible! I was so uncomfortable and happy all at once!

The race started quite abruptly at 6:00 am, and the temps warmed up to a balmy 50 degrees. The only thing colder than the temps was the occasional message that one of the locals spray painted on the road for the benefit of the runners, about every 30 feet or so, for the first few miles. The messages started out (in neon orange) saying things like, "Go Away" and "Get Lost!" After running over a few of them, they got a little more graphic, and actually made the people who paid any attention to them laugh hysterically. I don't think that was the effect the person was trying to elicit...but whoever sprayed those messages on the street obviously had no idea about running and clearly didn't have a good grasp on the mindset of endurance runners.

That person was also the only bad apple who tried (and failed) to spoil the whole bunch because everyone else on the course - spectators, volunteers, and runners - were all so warm, friendly and welcoming.

Even the horses up in the canyon seemed to watch the race with intrigue and a welcoming presence. One of the horses had his head propped up on the fence, and I watched him, standing there comfortably at his post, as we ran by in what had to be - in his eyes- a confusing mass of weirdos in bad outfits. If horses had chins, he would have been resting his on that fence post so that he wouldn't miss a single minute of the "worst parade ever" that immediately followed the "worst bonfire party ever."

The little town that we started in, called Wallsburg, Utah, is home to only 274 residents and was the beginning of the over 1,700 feet gradual descent in what many people would like you to think of as an all downhill marathon. It's a pretty steep, quad-crushing downhill, but there are most definitely some major "rollers" thrown in there for good measure. (That, and some serious wind. Oh yeah, and some extremely dry air that chaps your lips and makes you feel like a sponge out of water.) But it was so dang pretty!

For about seven miles or so, we ran along the gorgeous Deer Creek Reservoir, which is an amazingly beautiful lake up above Provo Canyon. They said that the local wildlife included mountain lions, hawks, turkeys, moose, deer, fox, and beaver. That made me chuckle, not so much because I didn't see any of these creatures, but mostly because my maturity level is lower than the moisture level in the Utah air.

As we made our way down the Provo Canyon, I came upon a group of firefighters running side by side, in full gear! It was so inspiring to see them running in their helmets, fire jackets and pants, and I thought about how difficult it would be to complete a marathon wearing all of that heavy stuff. It was really incredible, so I took a quick picture of them before passing them with a quick, if not awe-inspired, "hello."

The course ran along the Provo River for a while, and past the Sundance Resort. I didn't have a chance to say "Hi" to Robert Redford, but I did take a moment to think to myself: "What if?"

What if the documentary being made about Girls with Sole, called "Finish Line" is actually shown at the Sundance Film Festival one day? It doesn't seem all that far-fetched as I began to encounter more than a few coincidences or "signs" on the rest of the marathon course. Optimism is about seeing the possibilities and believing in a bright future, while actively pursuing personal goals.

Sign number one: I had to pee around mile 4 or 5, so I stepped into a Porta Potty. The first person I literally ran into was a woman named Sandy, who I met while running in the New England Challenge Marathon Series only a few weeks before! I like to affectionately refer to her as Sandy Cheeks (like the squirrel on *Spongebob Squarepants*) because, just like the cartoon squirrel, her name is Sandy, she's from Texas, and she's super smart and adorable. The timing was incredible! It was almost as if we had planned to meet there, and if we had, we still couldn't have pulled that off.

Sandy and I ran together for the next 12 miles or so. We chatted like old friends as we passed Vivian Park, where the 16-mile railway between Vivian Park and Heber

City is located. The railway is actually called the Heber Creeper and is now a non-profit organization that served as the "Olympic Steam Team" for the 2002 Olympics. (Is it just me, or does the Heeber Creeper sound like an old guy in your neighborhood that gives all the kids the Heebie Jeebies?) Seriously, stay away from the Heeber Creeper, kids!

At mile 17 or 18 (basically just before Sandy and I began to part ways, as fellow runners often do when one person is feeling great and one has most definitely had better days), we came upon the double waterfall called Bridal Veil Falls.

It was said that the falls cascade over 600 feet down into the Provo River, but on race day, it was a trifle more like a trickle than a cascade. Nonetheless, I was excited about it and asked Sandy to take my picture with the waterfall in the background. I had been carrying my phone the whole way for just this reason and wasn't going to let the lack of water pressure "dampen" my spirits.

(Insert the second "sign" here!) I stopped in the middle of the street...she snapped my picture, and we both went on our ways. I wasn't feeling great and had a lot of lower back pain, whereas Sandy was having a great day and ran ahead. Later, after the race, when I had a chance to look at the pictures ...I couldn't believe my eyes! The picture Sandy took of me looked as if a sunbeam was shining down from heaven, casting a single, golden spotlight on my head. It looked as mystifying and eerie as the Heeber Creeper sounds. I really felt like it was yet another sign that Girls with Sole is on an unstoppable train to reach girls in need of our programs no matter where they are!

I guess that must have been what was carrying me along, unbeknownst to me, as I made my way to the mouth of Provo Canyon and began to enter Mount Timpanogos somewhere near mile 19. My back was starting to really scream at me, and I wasn't feeling great, but knew

I would be able to gut it out and keep moving forward. I began to go through my thoughts of inspiration, such as the kids I work with, my husband and kids, and even my dog. I got choked up as I considered all the things I have been through in my life, as well as the hard times that many of the Girls with Sole kids have been through. Compared to much of that...this marathon wasn't shit. I thought about how simply completing the GWS program for many of the girls we serve feels as difficult to them as this marathon felt to me.

I began to feel the temps were getting higher and considered the last time I took in a Clif Shot energy gel and some water. It was time for more of both.

Then, like an oasis, the Clif sponsored rest stop was up ahead waiting for me. Yep...this was sign number three! But wait! There's more! I kept my eye on the prize and kept running until I was close enough to ask the two Clif reps working the tables which one of the flavors contained caffeine. (I always try to take the ones that have caffeine in them, to get a little more bang for my buck, so to speak.) There were three tables with three different flavors laid out on them. The third table was the only one that had caffeinated energy shots on it, so I beelined over there to grab one. Now you're not going to believe this... but that table was also the only one that also had a magazine laying on it. Out of all the magazines in the world, and all the issues of those magazines, which one do you think it was? It was the June 2014 issue of *Family Circle Magazine* that featured a story about Girls with Sole, complete with photos of me and some of the girls! I couldn't believe it! The Clif rep saw me putting my paws on her magazine, which I think also had her phone and her keys stuck in between the pages, and came over, smiling at me. The other rep followed her over as I exclaimed, "I'm in this!" They both looked at me funny and said, "no way!" I flipped to the page that the article was on and proudly held it up and said, "Girls with Sole, baby!!" The young lady looked at it and started to read it while saying over and over how incredible it was. I had the hugest smile plastered on my sweaty face, said, "that's me!" and continued on my way.

To make this "sign" even crazier, I need to fast forward a little bit - to four days after the race. On the Wednesday after the race, I was at home, working on Girls with Sole stuff, when I received an email from a producer at the NBC Today Show who also saw the article in Family Circle, and wanted to do a story on Girls with Sole!

There is pain in my heart at times for the girls I work with. The pain is empathy - not sympathy. It's pain I feel because I worry that I don't do enough for them, or that I'm not reaching enough kids who need Girls with Sole. Sometimes the pain creeps in to remind me that I'm human and although I'm not afraid to work hard, I become weary and feel like I'm just spinning my wheels. Sometimes, the pain disguises itself as fear, and sometimes it presents itself as failure to succeed in ways that I would like to. But no matter what form the pain comes in, I know that I will always keep moving forward and that forces - that go way beyond me - are pointing me in the direction that is to be. But most of all, I know in my heart and my soul that everything I do for Girls with Sole is "pain that I enjoy."

The last two tricks I have up my sleeve will require some audience participation. Let's concentrate on being grateful and choosing to have a positive outlook. Optimism is a choice we all have, but to achieve it, you have to have gratitude for the things you already have in your life. In the past, I have seen many therapists - (I know, huge shocker, right?!) - some of whom were really bad at their jobs. I believe that a bad therapist can be much more detrimental to a person's mental health than not seeing one at all. In the sea of horrible therapists that I have gone to, there was an excellent one whose advice was simple yet extremely impactful. She told me to keep a happiness or gratitude journal. Each day, I was to write down three things that made me happy (or that I was grateful for) on that particular day.

Focusing on those positive things each day took my mind out of its negative thinking patterns, and made me realize that no matter what, I could still move forward and find happiness. Life is beautiful if we are able to look at it through the lenses of optimism, love and gratitude. We need to embrace each emotion, each person, and experience because they're all here to help us become wiser and stronger.

Each pain serves its purpose - even if you don't know what the purpose is right away. So, with the right mindset, you can even be grateful for the tough times. For instance, if I hadn't been sexually abused as a kid, I wouldn't have created Girls with Sole, which is changing the lives of so many girls in need. Consider the things you are grateful for in your life - both positive and negative.

List at least 10 of them here, and also think about starting
your own, separate happiness/gratitude journal.

1. _____
2. _____
3. _____
4. _____
5. _____
6. _____
7. _____
8. _____
9. _____
10. _____

*" One of my core values is to help redefine what it means to be a
strong and beautiful woman in the music and fashion worlds and
to empower the wonderful things that make us unique."*
~ Janelle Monae

Finally, I want you to list all the reasons you rock! Why do you kick ass? We have been taught as women that self-love is boastful or even selfish. But, fuck that- cuz you rock!

So, this is your time to focus on all the positive things about yourself and how powerful you are. Think about how you would change the world by using your unique and amazing abilities!

In the space provided, create a list of your personal superpowers by writing at least 20 positive things about yourself.

You, my dear, are the house that R.O.C.K. built!

1. _____
2. _____
3. _____
4. _____
5. _____
6. _____
7. _____
8. _____
9. _____
10. _____
11. _____
12. _____
13. _____
14. _____
15. _____
16. _____
17. _____
18. _____
19. _____
20. _____

PART THREE
BUILDING AND CONSTRUCTION
(Courage)

"Find something you really care about and mix that with something you love doing." ~ Kathleen Hanna

I said it before, and I will say it again, to be a one-woman revolution, it's important to focus on our abilities, strengths and passions - to gain confidence and courage from those things - and let that confidence spill into all areas of our life. This is how courage is built. I think the best way to be a courageous one-woman revolution (other than being afraid of something and simply doing it anyway) is to build upon our passions. It's vital to build upon and actively nurture the Mission Statement you created earlier in this adventure- because I'm guessing that's where your passions reside.

Something I've noticed that really kicks ass, is that a person's passions can actually ignite other people's passions as well. This brings positive energy into, not only our own lives, but into other people's lives as well.

Think of being at a concert - and the energy that's produced by the singer, the band, and the crowd around you. When I was young, back in the Stone Ages, we lit torches at concerts and held them high above our heads, to show the band that we were moved by their music and badassery. Okay, they weren't torches- they were lighters- which have now been replaced by cellphone flashlights. Regardless of what light source is used at a show, the example still holds true. There's a ripple effect of energy produced that's truly euphoric.

Passion is what drives us forward from the energy it produces, and with it, comes the courage to pursue our goals and dreams.

There's an expression that says 'we get lost in the things we love, but we find ourselves there as well'. I can't agree with it more. I also believe we find our courage, purpose and voice when we find ourselves. In essence, I have found both myself and my life's purpose, in running. It's a passion that has given me many gifts and granted me with the courage to share these gifts with girls in need. Like a genie in a bottle, your run will grant you what you need.

There is a strong connection (and sometimes a very big difference) between running with your legs and running with your heart and soul. A run isn't just done physically, it can also cause you to psychologically run the gamut of your emotions, at times when you least expect it.

There are days when you squeeze a run in when you can, and it suits no other purpose than to get in some mileage, get home, showered and on with the rest of your day. As if this isn't enough of an accomplishment all on its own.

You've got things to do and the unemotional run, although energizing and fulfilling, is just something you do right before the next place you need to be.

Then there are those runs that help to jump-start your mind, like jumper cables on a car battery. These are the highly productive runs that can make you feel like an Olympic athlete, mom of the year, and CEO all rolled into one. A mental house cleaning run enables you to get inside your head and visit each room one-by-one, prioritizing and creating mental to-do lists. These runs are pretty awesome and always bring about a huge sense of accomplishment because you feel like you not only got your run in, but you simultaneously sorted through your life's worries and changed your mental to- do's into actual to- done's. No list is too great when you're high on Endorphins. You can do it all. Bring it on, world.

Occasionally, I even have a run that I would consider to be a serious training run. These are the runs where the entire time my legs are moving, and my heart is pumping hard within my chest, I'm concentrating on an upcoming race and mentally preparing myself for how I might feel on race day. These runs are comprised of mental body scans, connecting directly with every twinge or ache that might be talking to me and sending little warnings from my hip or Achilles to my brain. I go inside my head and think about what race day may bring- the mileage that day, the heat or weather, and how I will feel in my head, and my stomach, and, of course, crossing the finish line.

Then there are the emotional runs. The ones that feel like I'm the only person on the planet, and my legs feel powerful and strong but my mind is a blank canvas – until I hear a certain song on my iPod, or a very emotionally charged thought pops into my head and stays there like a cement kite. The thought runs with the rhythm of my legs and moves me emotionally, often evoking tears that make my even breaths feel like exercise-induced asthma. I can count on one hand how many times I have burst out into an audible sob while I was running. Recently, I added one more of those to the total count on my virtual Abacus.

The weather was cold, so I had to psyche myself up to go outside to run. Often, these end up being my best runs – much like the nights when you don't want to go to a party, but you tell yourself you'll only stay for an hour, and end up staying until 2:00 a.m. I stepped out into the crisp, early January air with the hope of getting a 30-minute post-holiday mental house cleaning run, but ended up with an emotionally driven and empowering 90-minute run instead.

At about 20 minutes into the run, I began to feel taller with my posture and legs somehow elongated. As my legs turned over, they actually felt like machines set to auto-pilot. I wasn't cold anymore, and everything seemed right in the world. Even the sun came out, causing me to squint like a happy, rebellious Vampire. My iPod was set to shuffle because I like my music to surprise me and to see how my body reacts to the random eclectic playlists that are chosen for me. When Swedish House Mafia's "Don't You Worry Child" played in my ears, I was instantly transported into my soul. I felt that the song was not only written for me from my father but that it was specifically chosen for me to hear today- while my mind, body and soul had its full attention, and could properly receive its message.

As a child, I had some trauma that I didn't deal with

properly, and as a result, there were some pretty dark times in my life as a young, blossoming adult. I was a hothouse flower with a hot head, trying to survive in an (often self-imposed) cold world. I never felt sorry for myself, which is a good thing, but there were some out-of-control years that I'm not proud of, with the period between age 21 until about 28 among my worst. These were the years that the anger, self-hate, and feelings of worthlessness reared their ugly head, and I was given the choice to do the work and slay the beast or to become the beast. I was admittedly scared. It was extremely frightening to think about where my life was going to end up, and to face the long road of confronting my inner demons, and forgiving those who wronged me while learning to love myself. These were daunting and seemingly impossible tasks at that time.

The only person who always stood by me, even at my worst, was my dad. He was my rock, and he always told me that heaven had a plan for me. He used those words. He believed in me when no one else did and constantly told me that I didn't need to worry. My father is no longer alive, but his love for me (and the messages he wishes to remind me of) are often placed in my heart while I'm running. This time, I heard it loud and clear, even though I keep my iPod volume way too high, and I burst into a sob. My legs just kept going (while my breathing was chopped to bits), choosing to ignore the cries, as if they had their own set of earbuds with the volume cranked too high.

The tears weren't all about me, however, and the message was two-fold because it brought to light the many emails, phone calls and conversations that come from so many of my girls in Girls with Sole. They often tell me how scared they are; how out of control their lives feel; and how they fear their feelings of worthlessness or ugliness will never go away.

It's now my turn to be the rock and to let them know there is a plan for them. The plan is to show them that there are people in their lives that care and that I know things can seem hopeless, but if you take care of yourself and stay healthy and strong with exercise and hard work–anything is possible. The plan is for me to be there and to bring Girls with Sole to them so that they can bring themselves across life's many finish lines. "Don't you worry child, see, heaven has a plan for you."

By getting lost in music, art, fitness, nature, philanthropy or whatever it is that you're passionate about, you will begin to discover the courage needed to build and construct your design for change, for being who you are, who you want to be or for chasing and attaining the life you want. Answer the following questions and then list the songs that move your soul on your Playlist.

POWERED BY PASSION
Answer the following in the space provided:

What are the things you wish you were doing instead of the things you have to do?

_____
_____
_____
_____

What inspires you?

_____
_____
_____
_____

What are some new experiences you would like to try?

_____
_____
_____
_____

What topics do you want to talk about and share with friends?

_____

_____

_____

_____

What do you dream about?

_____

_____

_____

_____

Make notes of the things that fill you with energy and excitement:

_____

_____

_____

_____

PLAYLIST - WHAT MUSIC MOVES MY SOUL:

List songs that move you, or fill you with positive energy and emotion.

1. _____
2. _____
3. _____
4. _____
5. _____
6. _____
7. _____
8. _____
9. _____
10. _____

Seldom does life slow down long enough for us to cognitively recognize if we are living it openly - approaching it with our arms, our hearts and our souls open; unafraid to take chances; unafraid of success or of failure, and unafraid of the opinions and perceptions of others. Seriously, who has time to think about that psycho-babble bullshit? Our days are so jam-packed, they tick by faster than a hummingbird's heart rate.

In my older age, however, I've come to realize the importance of taking the time to do exactly that. I find that I need to not only think about being open, but to actively work on being open, in order to unleash the courageous superhero within. By nurturing an open-minded and positive outlook, we can foster tenacity and courage.

The longer we experience the world, the more it can seem like there are millions of factors working against our openness. Failed relationships, heartache, trauma, and fear can leave us consistently bracing ourselves emotionally - shrinking away from meeting new people, goals and experiences much like our pupils shrink when we emerge from a dark movie theater into bright sunlight.

As an adult survivor of childhood sexual abuse, and even dating and domestic violence, my heart was closed down tighter than Fort Knox for a very long time. I built a fortress around it to keep it safe, and to ward off exposing what I felt was ugly, weak or shameful about myself. Like a crouching child hugging her knees into her chest, I provided myself with a false sense of security by staying as small and as closed as possible.

The more I travel, the more open I become. The more chances I take, the less fearful I am to try. Living wide open is like standing on a cliff overlooking the ocean - with your arms flung open wide, your face tilted to the sky, torso extended. Your body is open to all the elements, and nothing is protected. In this position of vulnerability, you are exposed to stressful winds and the raining down of sadness, insecurity or betrayal that can erode your self-esteem and confidence. If you remain open and wholeheartedly authentic in your stance, however, you will begin to feel the sun envelop your skin like a hug. Joy kicks your fear to the curb and welcomes in self-love, love from others, and the positive things that life can bring.

I love this quote by C. Joybell C.

"The only way that we can live, is if we grow. The only way that we can grow is if we change. The only way that we can change is if we learn. The only way that we can learn is if we are exposed. And the only way we can become exposed is if we throw ourselves out into the open."

During my 50 States for Sole marathon campaign for Girls with Sole, I participated in the Bear Lake Marathon Challenge, which meant that I would be running a full marathon in Idaho on a Friday, and another one in Wyoming on Sunday of that same weekend. There was an option to run one in Utah on Saturday as well, but I had just completed the Utah Valley Marathon, and didn't feel the need to duplicate the state - or the pain - so I skipped a day. I still spent plenty of time in Utah, however, since I had to fly into Salt Lake City and drive a rental car to the area in Idaho where I would be staying. The morning after I arrived in Utah, I woke with newly formed calluses on my hands from the death grip I had on the steering wheel of my rental car.

Due to some seriously delayed flights in both Cleveland and Denver, I didn't reach Salt Lake City until much later than I had planned. The rental car agency was somehow backed up at 11 pm and had me wait for my reserved and pre-paid vehicle for over 40 minutes. The longer I sat there waiting for my car, focusing on the almost 3-hour drive I still had in front of me to get to Montpelier, Idaho - the further away that little city seemed to be.

I sat down next to a teenager fiddling with his phone while his dad got the bad news about his own rental car delay. When his dad sat down, we started to chat, and of course, I ended up telling him about Girls with Sole and why I was driving to Idaho on my own in the middle of the night. His name was Sidney, a personal trainer from Texas who was in Salt Lake City with his 16-year-old son for a football camp that would expose him to top talent scouts and college coaches. We friended each other on Facebook and wished each other good luck in our endeavors. I have already heard that his son was one of the top contenders at camp, and he knows that I made the drive safely to Idaho.

When they finally called my name letting me know my car was ready, I jumped up and ran to the Hertz counter, steeling my mind in preparation for the long drive ahead. Within the first hour, I could feel the darkness of nothingness around me as I drove on twisting and turning mountain roads. It was thrilling and also petrifying to make this trip completely veiled in darkness and unknown territory- adrenaline was the only thing keeping me awake.

I was quickly learning that there's something about Idaho that makes you feel like you're the only person left on Earth - but in a good way. I didn't know it in the dark, but it's so lush, wide open, rugged and raw. I can't help but think about the movie "My Own Private Idaho" where two friends embark on a journey of personal discovery that leads them to one of the character's hometown in Idaho.

I continued to drive until my bladder simply wouldn't allow me to go any further. With absolutely nothing and nobody around but open wilderness, I pulled over onto gravel and dust and got out of the car to pee.

It's pretty cliché - but I couldn't believe the expanse of the sky, and how breathtakingly huge and crisp it was. I was frozen under what seemed like millions of white Christmas lights - each one flirtatiously winking at the

Milky Way that bobbed and weaved a roller boogie dance through the middle of the inky, black sky. I stared up from my squatting position of the tail end of the little Nissan Versa, trying not to spray my own shoes in my astonishment at the beauty and openness. I was awake now, and in full recognition that the adventure had officially begun.

I got back into the car and kept moving forward in the dark, which felt a bit like jumping off the high dive in the darkness of night, with the hope that nobody has drained the pool. It felt scary, but I had to trust and take that leap, knowing that I would eventually plunge into warm and pleasant water. When darkness surrounds us, it can intensify our feelings of loneliness, fear and even of being lost, but if we stay open, we can move forward in the comfort of knowing that the sun always comes up.

The next day revealed much more than callouses on my hands. In the bright sun, I could see what an incredibly beautiful place I was in and felt humbled by the majestic surroundings no longer hidden from view.

It's okay to let yourself feel scared, but it's important to move forward anyway. Believing in yourself and your motivations are portals to both self-discovery and living openly. We can gain much happiness and self-discovery if we allow it in. Dwelling on, and in, the dark blocks the beautiful view that surrounds us. It isn't that the beauty has gone away - we just have to hold on long enough for the darkness to pass in order to see it and appreciate it. When I travel and take chances with new challenges and physical goals, I let in the light that can guide and comfort me the next time I find myself in the dark.

A full day of exploration, and also picking up my race packet, lay before me. I drove through two or three towns in all of 10 minutes. The towns are very small with mountains and sky stretching around them like giants doing yoga. Montpelier, Idaho stirred memories of old Brady Bunch episodes when the Brady's stayed in a ghost town on their way to the Grand Canyon and when Bobby's newfound idol was Jesse James.

I drove through the small towns taking in as much as they could offer and watched the cows and horses do their thing on both sides of the road. Making my way through the Cache National Forest, windows down as I belted out an Air Supply song to one of the only radio stations I could get, was a far cry from the wide-eyed, yellow and white-knuckled drive I did a few hours earlier.

Bear Lake Marathon in Idaho was state 35 and Bear Lake Marathon in Wyoming was state 36 of my 50-state goal. I completed both of them with one day in between. They were both so amazing and fabulous. I couldn't help running with the perma-grin of a stoner. As I ran, I kept flinging my arms out to each side, like I could hug the gorgeousness that surrounded me and gather it towards me, pulling it into my heart. I couldn't believe how amazingly beautiful it was, and I wanted to absorb it all like a sponge.

Bear Lake Marathon Idaho is my new favorite course - but if you like crowd support you won't agree with me. Who needs spectators when the indescribable beauty of the course is enough to motivate you for days?

The nickname for the area we ran in is the "Caribbean of the Rockies," and Bear Lake upheld its reputation with water as blue as my daughter's eyes. We ran along dirty and dusty trails, and roads lined with curious cows and horses. I even saw two bald eagles and the nest they created on a power line. I met amazing people and chatted with two women I was destined to meet - both from Utah. One was a pacer in the marathon named Karrie, and the other was a social worker named Kaylee who worked for Children and Family Services. I talked to both of them about Girls with Sole and other things as well. We have already friended each other on Facebook, and I sent Kaylee copies of my book to give to any girls she works with whom she thinks might benefit from receiving it.

It felt pretty incredible to know in my heart and soul that I was literally on the path I'm meant to be on - and that when I'm open - that path can be awe-inspiring and amazing.

The marathon in Wyoming was equally as incredible, and I found myself saying out loud, "Can you believe this shit?!" as I ran down the long, wide open road - to no one other than myself. I couldn't believe it, and I ran along smiling the whole way, picturing scenes from Forrest Gump when he "just felt like running." I was giddy with openness. I wanted to be a cowgirl. I wanted to bottle the way the air smelled and the vastness of the sky and take it home with me. Running can have this effect on a person in any old place, but something about the wild, open beauty of the West creates an added sense of unabashed joy and of living wholeheartedly. Your inner child lets go of her knees and runs free and happy down the big expanse of road ahead and through her life......because it rocks!

"There's not one thing about Girl on Fire that's like any of my others. I'm in a totally new state of mind...This album is like saying I am who I am, not who you want me to be." ~ Alicia Keys

Before every Girls with Sole session, the entire group recites the Girls with Sole Creed to bring us together on the same page and start with power and courage. The Girls with Sole Creed goes like this:

We're Girls with Sole, and we're on the move
We're strong and proud, you can't stop our groove
We know who we are and who we want to be
We sail through life with resiliency
At Girls with Sole we set goals and believe
If we keep lacing up—we will always achieve!

Consider line three of the Girls with Sole Creed: "We know who we are and who we want to be" and what it means to you in terms of your individual strengths and qualities...now and in the future. In order to construct our design and build the courage to rock the house, we need to openly look at, and embrace, our plans for building upon the qualities we don't feel we have fully developed yet, but would like to work towards.

List your answers under each heading. Be sure to include at least 5 answers for each one.

We Know Who We Are (my strengths now)

1. _____
2. _____
3. _____
4. _____
5. _____

And Who We Want to Be (strengths I want to develop)

1. _____
2. _____
3. _____
4. _____
5. _____

PART FOUR
ROCKING IT OUT
(Killing Stereotypes)

"I grew up in a world that told girls they couldn't play
rock 'n' roll." ~ Joan Jett

Let's take all the awesomeness we've discovered about ourselves, put it into action, and rock that shit out!

"Don't lose your passion or the fighter that's inside of you"
~ P!nk

For so many reasons - most of which are pretty fucking obvious - I have loved the singer P!nk and consider her to be a badass, one-woman revolution. P!nk has always - and still continues to - kill stereotypes and resist conformity. During a time when cookie-cutter pop stars were being churned out on an assembly line, and everybody believed that you had to look a certain way to be successful in the music industry, P!nk was a one-woman revolution. She stayed true to herself, along with her immense amounts of talent, and has had enormous long-term success by doing it her own way. I love that she's an amazing example and role model for young girls and that she never needed to "define" herself. Her talent, passion, attitude and abilities ascend beyond mainstream music's ideal of the perfect pop star and cause her to rise above any one definition or label. Maybe there is some extra symbolism in the high-flying, strong and athletic acrobatics she performs during her concerts?

It's about being alive and feisty and not sitting down and shutting up. Even if people would like you to." ~ P!nk

I want every woman or girl to take this to heart. Killing stereotypes is the essence of being true to yourself and who you are - not who someone says you should be. After all is said and done - we are all we've got... and we only have one life to live. Therefore, living it our own way- without compromising who we are - is the only way we can continue to break barriers, expand opportunities for ourselves as women, and to wipe out the labels, the sham-

ing and the stereotypical idealistic ways that still exist today...as if this is still the fucking Stone Ages.

*"I wish for women to stop apologizing for those things that make
us women." ~ P!nk*

I'm told all the time that I don't look I was in foster care. It
makes me wonder: what does that look like? While we're
at it...what does a rape survivor look like? How about
someone with PTSD or mental illness? What does domestic violence look like? Or adoption? Do I look like any
of those? One of my favorites is when people tell me that
my looks - or aesthetics - don't match what comes out of
my mouth. Soccer mom on the outside- tugboat captain
or truck driver on the inside.

Recently, I posted a picture on my Facebook page of a
new tattoo I got on my back of Gustav Klimt's paint-
ing, *The Kiss*. Almost immediately following that post, I
received a private message from a dude I don't know very
well that said - "You don't seem like the tattoo type." My
answer was this: "Then I guess I don't seem like the type
to get my clit pierced - but I had one of those for five
years." (Made it difficult to ride the bike for long distanc-
es.)

...Crickets.

"Get comfortable with being uncomfortable." ~ *Unknown*

I'm going to say something else here that, more than likely, would not be said by any serious runner...ever. Are you ready? Here it is:

Sometimes it's my slowest races that I am most proud of. Many hardcore runners would shrink back, aghast, at such a statement. I suppose, by most people's standards, I'm a hardcore runner - evidenced by my completion of five Ironman Triathlons (2.4 mile swim, 112 mile bike, 26.2 mile run), 70 full (26.2 mile) marathons - including one in all 50 states, as well, as on the Great Wall of China - and zillions of other races. However, my way of thinking, in both running and life, has never reflected the quintessential or conventional thought process of, well, most human beings, let alone the mindset of a super hardcore, competitive runner. In the movie *Dirty Dancing*, we learned that you couldn't put Baby in the corner. If you spend any time with me at all, you may also learn that you can't put Liz in a neat little box. It's just the way it is.

I sat in the airport in Rochester, MN after completing my 48th marathon - and my 34th state of my 50 States For Sole campaign (my fundraising and awareness building campaign to run a full marathon in all 50 states for Girls with Sole) in the city of Winona earlier that morning. The Rochester airport looked like a library from the 1970s. There were only a few gates, and the entire place was devoid of travelers other than myself and two other women. My stomach was bugging me, my eyelids were as heavy as X-Ray aprons, and my left ass cheek had a Charley Horse big enough to accommodate John Wayne himself. The weekend before, I had run a marathon in Newport, Oregon and a week before that, I ran one in Denver. A week later, I would be doing a marathon on Friday in Idaho and another one on Sunday in Wyoming.

50 States For Sole was ticking by at an incredible pace. At times, I longed for home and my family, and my body felt the mileage the way it might if I were, say, hit by a bus - but I wouldn't have traded it for the world.

This challenge - and the entire Girls with Sole mission - is what I'm meant to do. It's my belief that I was put on this planet and endured some of the darker times in my life to bring my mission to fruition. The fact that it can be extremely challenging, and it hurts sometimes, exemplifies the true nature and spirit of not only endurance running but the core message of what I try and teach my Girls with Sole kids. It's not always going to be easy, but we can all move forward with perseverance, optimism, and resilience - in running and in life. We can get comfortable with being uncomfortable - and use it as a source of inner strength and mental toughness when we need it the most.

No one is impervious to a little bit of self-pity now and then, but a Girl With Sole and an endurance athlete uses her life experience and wisdom to squash it before it gets big enough to do any real damage to her spirit.

Sleep at the Super 8 the night before the marathon in Minnesota didn't come easy. It was as if my dingy surroundings made my family feel even further away and felt like the crappy hotel gave me permission to feel sorry for myself.

I woke at 3:45 am to the unwelcome sounds of an alarm and the loud rapping of rain on my hotel window... both of which could have exacerbated those feelings of self-pity. But I got up, got dressed and went down to the lobby to grab a coffee - and what I like to refer to as a cherry poppin' garbage bag. It's hard to believe, but in over 20 years of endurance racing, I had never worn a garbage bag to stay warm and dry. Well, there's a first for everything, so I grabbed that garbage bag offered by the Super 8 front desk guy, cut a hole in it for my head, and set out into the darkness, reminding myself that this marathon is something that I GET to do and that I WANT to do. 50 States For Sole was certainly a challenge, but I've experienced much worse in my life than running 26.2 miles in the rain.

For the most part, I would say that I actually embraced the challenges presented by my 50 states marathon goal. I kind of reveled in the adventure while simultaneously longing for home and my family each time I left for a race. It's a whacky dichotomy of bohemian and homebody all rolled into one. What can I say? I'm a complicated and complex individual who can't be categorized. Just when you think you can put me into a certain box, I'll surprise you (and myself) with a vulnerability never seen, or an extreme boldness that is equally unexpected. I've learned over the years that this is me and that it's okay… awesome, even. In the past, I used to wish that I was a simpler and easier person, and inwardly condemned myself for being so different. But now, I fully embrace my hippy-earthy-boho-anxious-loud-quiet-brave-nervous-Type A-over-achiever-slacker self-with extroverted and introverted tendencies - because it truly rocks to be who I am and to accept myself as I am.

After parking the car at the State Park and waiting for the start to go off for the 26.2-mile trail run, I mustered up my mental toughness and let the rain wash away any residual feelings of self-pity as I ran the first few loops in the dark. With each runner's stride, it got sloppy and muddy on the trail very quickly, yet I couldn't help smiling and having fun despite myself. The fact remains that I love to run and that overcoming obstacles and running with passion, heart and purpose is what this is all about.

In a short period of time, the heavy rain created havoc on the race course, causing dangerously slippery conditions. Too many runners were going down too many times, and I even saw one young lady in tears as she garnered supportive words of encouragement and hugs from her fellow athletes. In order to keep everyone safe, the race director changed the race course multiple times while we were running it! This was my second "first" of the day. As I have never worn a garbage bag before, I have never had a race course change while I was literally racing on it.

The course was a loop, so the race director was able to communicate the changes to the runners fairly easily. Upon completion of each loop, runners were required to pick up a rubber band from a table where race volunteers and officials sat and kept track of finishing times. Every time we reached the table, we would grab a rubber band, put it on our wrist, and head back out to do the loop again. With the course change, the number of required loops increased from 10 to 17, and we were taken off the trails, but I was happy to get out of the woods with all the thick, slick mud and onto the gravel and dirt road with surer footing. Races like this (when adversity is thrown at you, and things continuously change) serve as great reminders of the importance of resilience and being able to roll with the unexpected. It's also an amazing reminder that Lacing Up for a Lifetime of Achievement isn't just a tagline for Girls with Sole. A Girl With Sole digs deep, laces up and can rely on her ROCK solid foundation of Resilience, Optimism, Courage and Killing Stereotypes to keep moving forward and achieve her goals on the race course and in life.

It's my life's mission to be a living example and to show all the girls who need GWS that the Finish Line isn't the end — it's the beginning of what's possible. We can't control what happens to us and around us, but as Maya Angelou says - we can control how we respond to it.

It's in times like this that I'm glad I'm not your average bear, and I don't get too caught up in being brought down by "unfair" or uncomfortable conditions. Simply rolling with what you are given, staying positive, and focusing on the good can be so powerful and can help you see things in a different light.

It's also quite liberating and empowering to run

Garmin free for the pure, unadulterated joy gained from the rhythm of your feet and the movement in your heart and soul. (Another thing you probably won't hear from a hardcore runner - but I don't even own a Garmin.)

Happiness and pride shouldn't only come from the fastest times and swiftest course. Our slowest races can bring the biggest rewards because they were fought for and there is great pride to be had in truly earning that "Finish Line Feeling."

People forget the punk thing was really good for women. It motivated them to pick up a guitar rather than be a chanteuse. It allowed us to be aggressive." ~ Siouxsie Sioux.

Don't you ever let a soul in the world tell you that you can't be exactly who you are." ~ Lady Gaga

By now you know that you are a resilient, optimistic and courageous one-woman revolution who kills stereotypes daily by being exactly who you are - no matter what others may say, or what is expected of you because of irrelevant, outside factors. But what about those stubborn, persnickety self-imposed stereotypes?

We spend more time with ourselves in our own heads than we will ever spend with anyone else on the planet. That means it's very important to be kind to ourselves, and to consciously and continuously be our own best champion and superhero. Changing the way we see ourselves in the world as a female, student, mother, daughter, mom, boss, employee, athlete or otherwise, all starts in our head with the way we speak to ourself before it manifests and changes the way we present ourselves to the world.

We want to be sure we create the mold in the first place - before we choose whether or not we want to fit into it.

To ensure this is the case, I strongly suggest the use of positive self-talk in order to keep our superpowers for killing stereotypes in check. Just be sure not to dick around with hoping or wishing. If you want the changes to be real; the superpowers to hold true; and the molds to break like The Incredible Hulk was smashing them himself, you have to think of them as current or in the present tense.

We've all heard the expression "fake it 'till you make it.". In a sense, we need to continuously tell ourselves we're already in a place that we would like to be, and conduct ourselves accordingly until we actually get there. Especially if by society's (or our own) standards, we don't "belong" there.

As a one-woman revolution, I find that the more blunt I am with my personal positive statements, the more effective they are. For instance I replace negative self-talk about my body or my physical capabilities with: Fuck that! I'm strong, and my body can do amazing things. I'm an athlete, and I'm grateful for all the things my body can do..

When I'm discouraged about life or feeling down, I replace negative thoughts with positive, mega pep talks such as: Fuck that! I've got this. I'm resilient, confident, and have accomplished so much. I belong here. Nobody is me and I rock!

Believe me, whatever you tell yourself over and over again will not only become what you believe to be true, but also, what is actually your truth. Fuck what anyone else says if it's right for you in your heart and soul.

"Make the most of yourself by fanning the tiny, inner sparks of possibility into flames of achievement." ~ Golda Meir

In the space below, jot down negative statements and self-talk that you feel you need to overcome, and follow them with your own positive affirmations. Practice saying these positive affirmations to yourself until they become your real world .

_____

_____

_____

_____

_____

_____

_____

_____

_____

_____

_____

_____

_____

_____

_____

_____

_____

_____

_____

_____

_____

_____

_____

_____

_____

_____

_____

_____

_____

PART FiVE
VOICE OF SOLES

"And when that new day finally dawns, it will be because
of a lot of magnificent women, many of whom are right
here in this room tonight, and some pretty phenomenal
men, fighting hard to make sure that they become the
leaders who take us to the time when nobody ever has to
say, 'Me too' again." ~ Oprah

Sometimes all we want (and need) is to know that we're not alone. Feelings of loneliness and isolation can be so devastating to both physical and mental health and can lead to depression or unfulfilled lives. Under these conditions, healthy relationships, self-esteem and success in achieving fitness or life goals can begin to seem virtually impossible. I think part of the reason people love listening to podcasts, reading blogs or looking at inspirational posts and memes is because it's comforting, and feels good, to be able to relate to other people who are going through the same things that we are going through. No one wants to feel alone in their journey. It's motivating and uplifting to see that the things we fear can be conquered and that obstacles can be overcome. That mere mortals - just like us - can be superheroes and revolutionaries too.

The following essays have been written by Girls with Sole participants - or people whose life has been touched by Girls with Sole in some way - and who once believed they would never be able to change their lives for the better. They may have felt like a lost cause, misunderstood, forgotten, worthless, and at the end of their rope, but have become empowered by Girls with Sole and by giving voice to their stories. I believe sharing them here is the perfect way to pay homage to - and celebrate - the kickass warriors that they are: as well as to empower, inspire and encourage anyone who reads them.

We are many Soles but one Voice.
Please enjoy the following Voice of Soles.

"Owning our story and loving ourselves through that process is the bravest thing that we will ever do." ~ Brene Brown.

"No one can make you feel inferior without your consent"
~ Eleanor Roosevelt

"I'm writing about my life and how Girls with Sole has helped me. I never knew how to start something like this and I've finally figured it out. I'm going to start at the beginning.

I first started getting abused at the age of 6 on my birthday. I spilled pop on my dad's lap and he put me in my bathing suit and took off his belt and started hitting me anywhere he could. It continued throughout the years. I started drinking alcohol at the age of 8 with my friends, our first drink was redbull and vodka.

My family moved when I was 9 , and my sister was taken by my aunt due to the fact that she wasn't my dad's daughter - but he was abusing her too. I started rebelling against my dad and was sexually molested by 3 high school boys until we moved again. Things were fine for a month or two until my dad found my mom's escape plan and was enraged. My dad beat my mom in front of me with a metal hanger, so I ran outside and called my sister and exactly 6 minutes after I called 2 big trucks came in the driveway. These trucks had my sister, my cousin and like 5 of their friends. They tell me to call 911 and went inside to get my dad off my mama. By the time the police show up my dad is gone, the police put a warrant out for his arrest and he is picked up at work and released 4 months later. My parents get back together and it happens all over again and they still get back together.

For a few months things stayed non-abusive. Until my dad starts getting court papers about his ex-wife and he gets fired from his job, making his ager sky rocket. I come home from school on March 3rd 2014 and my dad is pissed. My dad walks in my room with my mom and grabs my hair and punches me twice. I begin crying and Boom! He hits me again. I, for the first time, hit him back. He gets more angry and continues hitting me and dragging me into the living room where he ends up breaking my nose. My dad goes to leave and I said to him "You are not going to be a coward and leave again are you?" He grabbed my hair, threw me to the ground and begins choking me until my mom pushed him off me. My dad stayed home that night and cut our phone cord. I went to school the next day and had to tell my counselor what happened. I couldn't exactly hide my black eyes, busted lip and broken nose. My dad was removed from home and my life by the courts for 5 years. Since then I grew into really unhealthy habits like doing drugs and having numerous sexual partners. I was, in my mind and everyone else's, trash and worthless, and treated myself that way too.

I was put in RTC and met Ms. Liz in the Girls with Sole group. This group has helped me so much with self respect and self esteem. Ms. Liz is fucking amazing. I found hope in Girls with Sole and realized I could get anger out by moving my body. We even boxed one day with real boxing gloves and it felt so good. One time we ran laps around the gym and every time we went by a long piece of paper that Ms. Liz hung on the wall. We would write negative things that people said to us in our lives. The whole sheet was full of horrible and ugly things. No one judged, we could be open and honest. Ms. Liz took the sheet down and held the paper with staff so we could run across the gym and bust through the paper football team style! Boom! It was incredible and so therapeutic.

Girls with Sole taught me I'm not what people said to me or what they did to me. I decide what my life will be and I'm worthy of happiness. I can do anything I put my mind to and don't have to rely on my next high to feel good about myself. I'm living a better and more healthy life and I'm happy about who I am."

Abigail, Age 16

> *"If I stop to kick every barking dog, I am not going to get where I'm going."* ~ Jackie Joyner-Kersee

So, my life has been one hell of a mess. I started out living with my mom and dad. We had a rundown 2-bedroom trailer. I don't remember much of life then, but from what I hear is that I was a happy kid living with two very unhappy people.

I remember bits and pieces of life after I turned three, my little brother was born. My grandma bought us a house so there would be enough room for all of us, the only catch was that my parents had to pay the bills and rent to my grandparents. The house was the best thing we could ask for. My mom was in nursing school, and my dad was a mechanic, so you'd think hey, they have it made. Well, that was true for a while. My mom found alcohol and lost her ability to pay the bills, my dad would give her money for the rent and things like that, and she went to the bar instead. After that, it fell apart, and it happened fast.

My mom dropped out of school, and we lived without electricity for probably two months. My dad's work transferred him to Youngstown, so we moved to Liberty, Ohio. We moved back into a trailer; we had just got out of a trailer two years before, only this time our trailer was in a rundown trailer park.

I wasn't the outgoing type, so I had a hard time making friends. After a few months of being there, school started, and I met my first friend at the bus stop. I was so happy because I finally had someone my age that I could talk to. She would come over, try to stay the night, then get scared and have to leave. I was probably six by this time, and my mom made me walk her home. One time, I got picked up by the police, and they took me home. I remember one thing he said that stood out to me, "If you're walking her home so she gets there safe, who's gonna walk you home to make sure you get there safe?" I still think about that. I worked up the courage to stay the night at her house.

I used to wish I didn't, but now it has all become a part of my story and made me stronger. That night was well...let me back up.

We were still struggling to make the bills because of my mom's habits, so I wanted to help and do anything to get money for my family. Around this time, my dad started beating me and my mom, so I was really looking for an escape. I worked up the courage to stay with her, and she knew about everything going on at my house so she was all for it. By this time, I was seven years old, I was too young to know any better and she and her dad promised me all the money I could ask for. He told me that he would help me buy my mom a house if I would let him and his daughter have sex with me. I was too young to know there was something wrong with that. He told me he was giving the money to my mom, so I went over to their house every weekend and let them do the dirty, nasty things to me that now I can't believe I let happen.

After about 6 months, they moved, and I was scared because I thought they were giving the money to my mom and if they left, I wouldn't be able to get away from my dad. My dad started working for our landlord fixing up trailers for extra money. He did this one trailer and afterwards, this guy kept saying that my dad stole his TV. So, this guy had a daughter who was 16, and she jumped me and almost killed me. After that incident, we moved to Newton Falls, and the beatings from my dad got worse, and he picked up drinking so it became lethal. My mom started cheating on my dad, and it was our ticket out of there. My parents got divorced, and we moved into another trailer park. This guy was a drinker too. He and my mom got more and more into alcohol, partying, and later on drugs. After a few months of them being together, he started beating my mom; we were back where we started. Just a different guy, different town, and another trailer park. One time I had to call the police or my mom would have died. He locked me in my room and was beating my mom. He went to the store to get more beer, and my mom slid her phone under the door and told me to get out and stay safe. Leaving my mom behind was so hard, so I didn't. I stayed. When he got back, he was more intoxicated than when he left. He came in and smashed all our TVs with a hammer and tried to hit my mom with it. That's when I called the cops, and they pulled my mom and me out of the house and asked if she would like to press charges ...then she said no. The officers told us to leave for the night so he could sober up. We went across the street until the police left and then we went back home. The house was trashed; there was cat litter dumped all over my bed, and even my animals were hiding. After that night, my relationship with my mom was never the same. He left her, and she blamed me. It was all my fault because I called the cops. We could no longer pay the bills and lost our trailer. I was at school when they threw all our stuff in the front yard. I got off the bus, and my stuff was everywhere, and they arrested my mom because she tried to lock them out. I didn't know what to do, so I called my grandparents, and they came and got me. When my mom got out of jail, they bought us another house and told my mom no boyfriends living in the house... and guess what? She didn't listen.

I was 13 when we moved into the new house, and life was a struggle. We were getting child support from my dad, and that was the only way we could pay our bills because my mom wouldn't work and had a bad addiction problem. I had to hide the credit card so she wouldn't spend everything before our bills were paid. I hid the card, and she beat me to get it back from me.

On my 14th birthday, I woke up and my mom was drunk; it was super early in the morning, and she was trashed. I went downstairs for breakfast, and she started screaming at me. Probably trying to show off for her new boyfriend I'm guessing, but I'll really never know. She came up behind me and smacked me in the side of the head. I turned and backed away, and she ran at me, and we started fighting while her boyfriend cheered her on.

She dumped a glass of vodka over my head and told me to pack my stuff and get out. I ran upstairs and locked my door. I started throwing my clothes in bags and throwing the bags out the window. I was in a tank top and shorts that day...January 29th...when I went downstairs, she grabbed me by my hair when I said I'd packed and threw me outside. I was on the front porch, and she sent her boyfriend outside to take my bags from me and put them in the trash can. She told me I deserved to be naked. I sat outside waiting for my aunt to come and get me, and my mom came out and asked me if I was cold. Then she dumped boiling water down my back. To this day, I don't understand why she did that to me, and I'll never understand.

I stayed with my aunt for a week and went back home. I started to develop my own "happy place" with alcohol, pot and sex. Now, looking back, I'm mad at myself for the messes in my life that I made. I was refusing school, staying home, drinking or doing whatever I wanted. Sometimes, I would say I was going to school, but I would go to Canton all day with my "friends" and steal from stores to get alcohol and stuff. I eventually got charged for not going to school and got caught stealing. When I got charged, I still wouldn't go. I ran away and stayed with a girl I knew, but my P.O. showed up one day and told me to pack for a few days' stay with my grandparents. It was a trick. My grandparents were given temporary custody. I didn't want to be there. I wanted to live at my mom's, but I don't know why. I ran away from my grandma's three times, so they put me in a place called Safe House. I was happy there for about a month, and then I got into a fight with this girl named Lilly, and after that, it was me getting restrained 2-3 times a week.

In October, Lilly died. I felt like shit and like it was my fault, so I ran away and was gone for 2 weeks, got caught, went back and then ran again. That second time, I didn't go back. I came to RTC.

I got here November 2nd. I told my story or at least parts of it so you could have a feel for who I am, or was. So you would have an idea on what I went through and what I needed help with.

Ms. Liz has been my biggest supporter throughout my whole stay here. Girls with Sole has shown me that I am awesome, I can do anything I set my mind to, and that no matter what my story is, who I am, I can't change it... but I can recover from it, and I can bounce back. I have accomplished all my goals since I came to RTC, and Ms. Liz Ferro has pushed me to strive for excellence and to become resilient. I always have counseling on Thursdays before Girls with Sole, and I'd come in, in a bad mood, and Ms. Liz would tell me to put a smile on my face and push me to want to do better.

Now, I'm leaving in a month. I have accomplished and made this program, and I made it because of Ms. Liz's push. If we didn't have Girls with Sole, I'd probably still be at the bottom of the food chain, waiting for the right thing to come along and take me with it.

Ms. Liz is my rock and foundation, the one I look to confide in. I sit around and wait for Thursdays with Ms. Liz. When I leave here, I'm going to live with my grandparents. They're giving me a second chance.

My dad has seven kids, and now I have visits with my brother who I mentioned previously. My mom has been in jail since October and is soon being transferred for treatment to SRCCC; she is actually willing to get help. The man who raped me is in prison because someone else turned him in. Everything has fallen into place in my life.

I'm getting a job once I get out, and I'm moving to South Carolina, and best of all, I get to go home with my family. I took Ms. Liz's advice, and I'm living better, and

I'm happy about who I am.

I've also read Ms. Liz's book like 10 times, and it's so inspiring. It makes me want to get off my butt and help everyone.

Thank you for giving me this opportunity to work with Ms. Liz and to let you know what I've been through, and a chance to tell my story. Some things in here have never left my head, I've never told anyone, so it feels good to be able to get it off my chest and put it where someone will acknowledge it. Thank you.

Kylee, Age 16

"You can break down a woman temporarily, but a real woman will always pick up the pieces, rebuild herself and come back stronger than ever." ~ Joy Vaal

Reclaiming The Girl

Sometimes, it takes a while to remember who you really are, to reclaim what was yours to begin with. For me, it took 25 years.

One day, when I was 12 years old, a neighbor whom I admired and trusted told me he wanted to show me how to be a woman. When I failed to follow his "lesson plan," he became violent. He choked me, raped me, and called me names I had never heard before. It was one afternoon in an otherwise ordinary life, but it changed me forever.

I told no one about it for over a decade. I was blessed to live in a loving home, and I enjoyed school, but I still suffered from my secret. Until he moved away, I was terrified that my neighbor would rape me again or kill me. I tried drowning myself in a nearby creek. I sniffed gasoline and chlorine bleach to help ease my anxiety, and when I felt especially bad, I would lightly burn the skin on my thighs with a lighter I had stolen from a friend's dad. Over time, these impulses toward self-harm faded, and I was able to escape into my studies and music. But what remained was a hatred for my body. I believed what my neighbor had told me, that I was dirty and disgusting. My body meant nothing to me.

Until recently, I only exercised if I felt the need to punish myself for being too fat or too lazy. (I hated exerting myself, and I really hated to sweat). But in June of 2014, thanks to a mutual friend, I learned about Liz Ferro and Girls with Sole, and I started running. I ran my first 5K a month later and read "Finish Line Feeling" shortly after that. I can't say that I fell in love with running (I still have days when I question the sanity of it!), but I did fall in love with the way it made me feel. A few months ago,

I joined a gym near my home to add strength to my new habit of running, and it has become my sanctuary!

I knew that I was a changed woman when one day at the gym, I looked in the mirror as I lifted weights, sweat pouring off of me, and I was not disgusted but delighted at the woman staring back at me. I now have a love for my body that I've not felt since I was a child. My body finally feels whole and free — something to be challenged and nurtured, not neglected or shamed. For so long, I've been chasing a remedy for the feeling of being disconnected from my body, and I have finally found that remedy in fitness. Not only am I physically and mentally healthier, but I am setting, pursuing, and reaching goals in all parts of my life that I would never have dared to even consider before. I am a 38-year-old woman, and I finally feel alive. I believe in the mission of Girls with Sole because fitness has enabled me to reclaim the girl inside who was stolen from me years ago. I believe in Girls with Sole because every girl is beautiful and special, and every girl deserves to feel whole and free — no matter how old a girl she is! We are all survivors.

One of these days, I plan to run a marathon of my own. When I do, as with other races, the feeling of accomplishment and elation in crossing the finish line will be summed up in two words: girl power.

Becky, Age 38

"I really think a champion is defined not by their wins, but how they can recover when they fall." ~ Serena Williams

Liz Ferro.....is a petite blonde lady who is loud, exciting, and so caring. Her aura is so strong that it mesmerizes everyone she comes in contact with. Girls with Sole is one of those blessed groups you only come in contact with so often.

With RTC, we attend too many groups to count within the 6 months you receive treatment. Girls with Sole is the only group I actually look forward to every week. It's not boring, it's not corny, and Miss Liz never has the same thing to lecture every group. She is so energetic and out-going, it's almost impossible to be sad around her. Any time I've had a bad day, week or even past hour, Miss Liz is willing to lift your spirits and help. You don't often run into someone so genuine. That's why knowing how Girls with Sole helped me and all the other girls is so beautiful to hear.

My whole life has been a hand of shitty cards. My dad has been in and out of prison, doing drugs and getting wrapped up in gangs. My mom is a stripper who did normal stripper "gigs" which led to a lot of drugs, abuse from sugar daddies; you name it. I didn't exactly have the dream childhood. When JFS was brought into the picture, I moved in with my grandparents. My grandma (the angry, disabled woman) and my grandpa (the rock star-guitar playing alcoholic) gave me a couple of good years and a couple of rough years. Their marriage fell apart, and it was taken out mostly on me. I was constantly told I would be my mom. Or a deadbeat like my dad. I never thought I would amount to much because it was engraved in my brain. The rest of my family turned a shy eye to the situation and told me to be grateful for what I have. I never knew the severity of the verbal abuse I was going through. I can remember the end of living with my grandma so clearly. Someone called child services when they got wind of what was going on. My grandma said she was going to make my life hell for ratting her out. In her eyes, I did this. I was the snitch, the scared shitless 15-year-old. I didn't see a rainbow at the end of this storm.

The only way out was to end it all. I told my boyfriend I loved him and I was sorry. Then I proceeded to write my suicide letter, loaded a gun, and just cried. All I could do was hold the gun and just stare at it. The next thing I knew, the cops were there, telling me I wasn't being abused. When they asked me why I wanted to die so bad, I remembered a conversation with my grandma where she told me she wanted me dead. So, that's what I told them. "Mr. Bad Cop" called me a liar and hauled me to a mental hospital. There, I failed a drug test for THC, various pills (uppers mostly), and other harder things we won't mention.

Yeah, I signed the D.A.R.E. paper vowing to "say no," but my history made it hard not to. By nine years old, I was drinking and smoking weed with all the older kids. I was like the "little sister." I only got into harder drugs as I got older. I remember being in an abusive relationship for three and a half years. Sexual, mental, and physical abuse weren't taught at school, so I didn't exactly know I was a victim of all three. I thought it was love. As I got older, I only dated his friends, who were exactly like my ex-boyfriend.

Moving on, not being allowed back at my grandparents, I moved in with my aunt and uncle. They were pretty normal. They fought a lot but really cared about me. I was already wrapped up in so much I couldn't get out of it. I was a regular pill-popper, Friday-Saturday night drinker, and an everyday stoner. They couldn't control me, so they kicked me out.

Here I am. RTC bound.

Here's the good part! My first day here was, in fact, a Thursday. That is the day we had Girls with Sole. I found salvation in exercise, sanity in the activities, and love in

Miss Liz. When I was so broken and beaten down, Miss Liz put me together piece by piece. I read her book which I related to. What? A cool adult who relates to me? Yes! My self-esteem would be a grain of sand if it weren't for this group.

I'm near the end of the program here at RTC. The courts asked me what I liked most at RTC and what helped me most. I knew EXACTLY what I wanted to say. Here was my response:

"Girls with Sole. There was a gigantic problem with learning to love me. Finding love (and a coping skill) in exercise made my heart so happy. Having someone come in and be so silly with me healed wounds I couldn't even look at. I'm so glad I was sent to RTC just to experience this."

Liz Ferro may be small, a little goofy, but she has had the most positive impact on my life anyone ever has. She's my spirit animal, a role model, and someone I want the world to know and love."

June, Age 16

My name is Adrienne. When I was 17, I was sent to the Residential Treatment Center. I was living a criminal lifestyle that at the time I did not realize was going to take me nowhere. Before I got caught up in the negativity and trouble, I was a very athletic, my favorites being soccer and track. I lost that somewhere along the way, blinded by the drugs, recklessness, and negative influences.

While I was in RTC, I was able to take part in the Girls with Sole program and met Liz Ferro. The light that shone within her and her loving soul opened my eyes back up to the positive lifestyle I once knew and loved. She gave me back the empowerment I used to feel before, and I soon realized why I loved sports and running so much.

Once I was able to complete the RTC program, I carried the light Liz brought back into my life with all I did. I have faced lots of obstacles along the way but thankfully, I know I have Liz's support, encouragement, and POSITIVITY that is essential to achieving my fullest potential. The impact she has made on my life is like no other. I have been very thankful for knowing there is someone out there who understands why I chose the path I did but encouraged me to see the good in all situations and gave me better techniques to get through the dark times.

Liz and I ran in a GWS event a few years ago (after RTC). Something sparked in me during that cold, rainy race. When I was running in the rain and cold, I wanted to give up, I wanted to quit, and I thought it wasn't worth it. Liz's encouragement and motivation kept playing in my head, and I started thinking about all the obstacles in the race (in my life). I knew I couldn't give up; I had to push through. There was so much more I had to accomplish. Liz believed in me to keep pushing and overcome, so I believed in myself! It is so easy to get caught up in life and the hardships that come with it, but it is an INCREDIBLE feeling to overcome something that has been holding you back, to achieve something for which you have been working for so long.

Running is the same way. It is so easy to give up, to take the easy route and not even start. It is a whole new world that women can hold in their hands and use to build themselves up. There is no other strength in the world like feeling you can't do something but ignoring it and BELIEVING IN YOURSELF and making it happen. This is the strength Liz has helped me find again and again.

I was in RTC five years ago and am now a happy mother of two beautiful children and have the career of my dreams. Our business mindset is very similar to the GWS morals. We only encourage growth, support, and POSITIVITY. We push everyone around us to fulfill their dreams and be the best we can be. I encourage everyone to become involved with Liz's program and take it to your heart. The light that Liz brought into my life will forever be a piece of me, and it continues to push me to be the absolute best I can be.

Thank you, Liz for all your love and support. That particular race day plays over in my head very often, and I love the power it gives me. I wouldn't be the mother or business woman I am today without you coming to me when I needed you the most.

Adrienne, Age 21

"When you are happy with who you are, it won't matter who isn't."
~ Stacie Martin

I used to be afraid. I used to be afraid of what people would think, of what I would see when I looked in the mirror, of what I had to go home to and what I might find when I got there. In fact, I used to be so afraid to go home that when I finally psyched myself up to put the key in the door, I'd turn around and run before my conscience told me to go back.

You may be thinking, "Mandi, running from your fears is cowardly and unrealistic."

That's what my counselor told me. She also told me that refusing to face reality is called "being delusional."

I called it having a Superpower. I fail to see the difference. When life sucks real bad, I could just leave whenever I wanted, like a magic trick, "wanna see me disappear?" Don't ask; I'll do it anyway to save you the trouble. Poof! I'm gone.

So, I bet you're wondering where I went when I ran from my fears. Well, I can tell you what places I didn't go: the library, school, my grandmother's, Joe's Crabshack, the grocery store, on a pilgrimage. Long story short, I didn't go anywhere innocent or family oriented.

My family was too high to care where I went or what I did. Then, I discovered drugs and had a new way to escape reality. I didn't even have to leave my house! Then, on one fateful evening, I was arrested. My family relinquished custody of me, and I was released to a foster family. My life spun out of control when I got out. I had a crazy, weird new family. New school, and eventually new drugs. My addiction finally came to light, and things got bad again. My foster family decided to move to Minnesota, and I was truly alone. I went to a group home, and two weeks later, I came to RTC. Later in the day when I got here, they told me to put on my own clothes for working out, and I thought, "Great, we're gonna be doing military drills or something, I just know it!"

We went down to the gym, and I was instantly greeted by Ms. Liz. My first thought was, "Who is this crazy hyper pixie lady?" but it turns out that Ms. Liz isn't just some pixie lady who shows up to work us out.

It reality, she's my Fairy God Mother. She took my shoe size and bra size, and I was instantly amazed by the amount of generosity a single woman can possess.

Over the past six months, Ms. Liz has done so much for me and every other girl here at RTC. She helped me shed my skin and learn to fly. Even after all the adversity I've been through, she has helped me turn into a beautiful butterfly. Ms. Liz has inspired me to turn my life into something better. I've seen the future, but through someone else's eyes. I've stepped through the looking glass and seen an alternate path. I'm so grateful and lucky to have the opportunity to meet Ms. Liz and participate in Girls with Sole. I know what I could be. I've seen what others have seen, and I am no longer ashamed of what the future holds.

I AM NO LONGER AFRAID.

Mandi, Age 16

"Stay in your heart. Make a home there. Not for another, but for yourself." ~ Betty Larrea

Welcome to my life. There's a lot of pain hidden behind my brown eyes, and there's a lot of rain covering blue skies. I'm sixteen now, but it feels like my childhood just flew by. I grew up with mental illness. Yet depression, PTSD and anxiety has never stopped me.

When I was thirteen, I knew what death was before I knew how beautiful I really am, but still to this day, insecurities consume me. I have always strived to succeed so when I do, I can look back, and I can thank God for all the trials and tribulations because those are my motivations.

I've lost a lot except the need to speak up and speak out about the terrible things I have seen while seeing all of the positive things in this world. I deserve to have everything that has been stolen from me.

If I could speak to my ten-year-old self, I would tell her that she is worthy of love and how God has not forsaken her. I would take her fears and write them on a piece of paper and set it to flames. I wouldn't take the things that have happened to me away because those are the things that have built the resiliency in me.

Girls with Sole, not only did you teach me to use exercise to cope, you taught me how strong I am, both mentally and physically. I can take any obstacle, pick it up and move it away from my goals. Ms. Liz showed me that no matter how big or heavy something is – I can lift it and lift myself. No matter what, nothing can stop me from achieving my goals.

I am a Girl With Sole.

Tavia, Age 16

"And when you realize that they're just thoughts, you will be free."
~ Sophie Grey

Hello, my name is Kerriah, and I would like to tell you how Girls with Sole has helped me because Mrs. Liz is just so caring, and loving. She inspires me. She taught me to accept people for who they are and accept me for who I am.

I am me. People are supposed to love me for me. In 20 years, I imagine myself helping MRDD kids or adults. I love helping them. They make me a better caring person and also Mrs. Liz. She is such an amazing woman. The reason I'm at RTC is because I ran from my problems, thinking that it would help. I disappointed a lot of people doing what I did. I have no idea what could have happened, but I could have ended up dead. When I was 15 years old, my best friend committed suicide. I don't really know why, but I sometimes feel like it was my fault because I hit him because we were fighting, and he told me he was in love with me.

This is why I love Girls with Sole. Since I met Liz Ferro, I just started being myself and started expressing my feelings. She always taught me to think positive and great things will come my way. I learned to be loving, caring respectful and most important, I will be myself. I'm not ready to be 18 years old. I believe it's gonna be hard. But I got to grow up sometime. I really put all my trust in Mrs. Liz. I think she's so special. She's a very gifted runner. I love her. I sometimes wish she was part of my family.

I think it's so great that grown-ups like Mrs. Liz actually care for troubled kids. It makes me smile when I think of it. She makes my day when she comes here. I pray for her in my prayers. I love her and her friends she brings. God Bless, and thank you for reading.

Kerriah, Age 15

"You can waste your lives drawing lines. Or you can live your life crossing them." ~ Shonda Rhimes

When I first came to RTC, my depression was the worst it has ever been. I was addicted to drugs and was overall a pessimistic person. On my third day, Miss Liz came. When the other girls told me how much they loved her, I started to immediately love her. I didn't even know what Girls with Sole was. But everyone was so hype, especially Miss Liz!

Here at RTC, not a lot of people are energetic or even happy. All the smiling, laughing, bonding, and exercising made me so happy, and I wanted to go so bad the next week. I had something to look forward to that was healthy and beneficial to me.

So, next week came, and Miss Liz had a Girls with Sole water bottle, her book, a sports bra, and even running shoes for me. I was sublime. These were name brand things, and Miss Liz was so happy to give them to me. I carry my water bottle with pride, wear my shoes comfortably, and carry a great deal of warmth in my heart thanks to Girls with Sole.

I read Miss Liz's book "Finish Line Feeling" the second she gave it to me. It made me feel a lot less alone. THE EXACT things I was doing and going through, someone experienced. Someone who made me inspired. I'm so grateful for this group and Miss Liz. She has made the biggest positive impact on my life that I've ever had in my life.

Destiny, Age 16

"When the whole world is silent, even one voice becomes powerful."
~ Malala Yousafzai

Depression isn't just something anyone can get over – overnight – or weeks – or months. It's a process that takes years because of all the time we've been put down.

Starting when I was a kid, I was abused and beaten by my father. I loved him after all that he put me through. Eight years of tears and pain. After that, my parents split. After that, my whole life changed. Everything got darker & more blurry.

My dad attempted suicide in front of me. It was the scariest thing to experience. I was nine, and I didn't know what to do, so I took the blame for it all. I believed it was all my fault because he hated me, even though I loved him. I started to understand things a little more a couple of years later at age 11, so things started to get better for me. Until I went to school again. I got bullied. I never told anyone because I thought it would make things worse than it already was. That's when I started to cut. Cutting was a way to escape this world and go to another.

At age 13, I was raped. I never told anyone for three years until I had a deep talk with my best friend. She's the only one I ever told. After that happened, I was never satisfied with who I was. I didn't feel like myself anymore. I felt so out of place. I didn't belong. And I still feel like I don't belong today.

Sometimes, I feel like suicide is the escape for everything. I attempted it a few times but never reached my goal of succeeding. What kept holding me back? I was never able to answer this question, and I still can't. Was it the thought of hurting my best friend? My family? The unknown world after death? The pain I would cause others? I still don't know, but I have an idea. It was God and my guardian angel. But then a wonderful young lady, Liz Ferro, entered my life. When I first heard of GWS, I told myself it was going to be stupid. Who cares what she went through? She doesn't know what I'm going through or what I have been through. I lied to myself. My first day doing GWS was a life changer.

Liz inspires me and many other young girls like me that no matter what you go through or where you come from, you can always succeed. Just keep moving forward. Reading "Finish Line Feeling" has inspired my life in so many ways. Exercising has been my way of relieving stress and stopping me from making decisions that I would regret — or doing anything that nobody could change. Liz inspired me to keep my head up and focus on what is in front of me.

Emily, Age 15

I love to see a young girl go out and grab the world by the lapels. Life's a bitch. You've got to go out and kick ass. ~ *Maya Angelou*

When I first came here, Liz was just a person. I thought she was paid to come in here and do this with us, and then I read Liz's book, and it gave me a way, way, way different perspective on her, and I think she's one of the most powerful women I know in my life because of what she's endured and how happy she is now these days. So, I look up to her and every single time I see her, I just look at her and study her, and think if she got through that stuff then I can, too, and I can change my life and break the cycle in my family.

Lexi, Age 15

"Be rebellious! When you accept who you are and like yourself un-conditionally, you start an inner revolution. Your world is waiting."
~ *Ana Barreto*

From the moment that we lace up our running shoes, we become Girls with Sole. We are able to forget, if only for an hour, our anger and pain. As we run or talk, it seems to magically melt away.

Girls who are fighting become friends. Girls who normally do not speak to each other suddenly are running side by side and laughing. Girls with Sole is somewhere safe where we are encouraged to be ourselves, and it is somewhere where everyone believes that we can do great things, even if we can't believe it ourselves. It is a place where we are free to discover that our pasts don't have to guide our futures and that we are stronger than we may think. Sometimes, it is simply a place to laugh and be a kid - without having to worry about everything that sur-rounds us every day.

Girls with Sole has helped me in many ways. It has given me friends, it has given me support, and it has defi-nitely given me a place to laugh and have fun. But it has given me so much more than that. It's given me a role model and support and belief that one day I can change lives like Miss Liz has changed mine. It has given me the chance to stop viewing my body as this ugly, fat, good for nothing thing and to see, instead, how I can make it run, and how if I treat it right, it can carry me across many finish lines. It has given me a healthy escape from the pain of my past and my present.

Before I was in Girls with Sole, I was pretty messed up. I'm not perfect now, but I can admit that no one is. I still sometimes feel like giving up and letting life just swallow me whole. But Girls with Sole is always there, something I can rely on. It is the finish line or the last lap, that thing that makes you keep going, even if, as you do, you are thinking to yourself that you are crazy. And it gets me through. I am able to go and release all the painful emotions that tear at me. I am able to see that people care, that I'm not alone, and that there is always hope.

When I started to write this, I thought I knew what I wanted to say, and I did know part of it. Everything I have written is true. But I think the most important thing I have gained from Girls with Sole and that I have seen others in the program gain is hope. A lot of us don't have very many people to encourage us, and we don't have many people to rely on. Girls with Sole encourages us, but it also teaches us to encourage ourselves.

Miss Liz, and all the other awesome people involved with Girls with Sole, are all very supportive. But, we learn our strengths and we see what we can do, and we start to believe in ourselves. We start to stop caring about the voices that cry discouragements and to listen to that soft voice deep inside each of us which is quietly shouting, "You can do it!" Girls with Sole has let me hear that voice, and to believe it.

Dezi, Age 16

"...To be true to myself, to be the person that was on the inside of me, and not play games. That's what I'm trying to do mostly in the whole world, is to not bullshit myself and not bullshit anybody else." ~ Janis Joplin

I remember that day when he came in and pushed me out of the way and said move out my way before "you get what you deserve." He started beating me because "I got on his nerves." He was beating on me having a blast while I remembered I had a baby on the way, but it was a little too late for my ass. The baby was gone, and I struggled to move on. I felt like ending my life. There was no more light.

Going through the pain and living my life in vain. I was so hurt by something I knew would never work.

But then one day, I saw a little bright light that told me I need to fight. When I did, I found out what the light was, and now I'm a fighter. I still have problems, but I don't hold onto them. Mrs. Liz changed my life and helped me stay strong, even in strife.

Girls with Sole taught me to see my strength, see my worth and fight no matter what the dirt.

I move on because life isn't always what it seems. So, I look up and I move forward, and I like being me and only me and living my life happily.

Thank you to Girls with Sole and Mrs. Liz for keeping the light within so I can go, fight, win.

Queen, Age 15

"Be strong when you are weak. Be brave when you are scared. Be humble when you are victorious. Be badass every day!" ~ P!nk

I don't cry. I most definitely do not cry in public, or in this case, in a room filled with peers. Suffice it to say that the words uttered by Liz Ferro did not fall on deaf ears. I must confess that I wasn't interested in hearing her speak in the slightest. My co-workers can corroborate that story. I whined, "You can't pay me to get on a treadmill, let alone be involved in athletics. There's no way anything this lady has to say will affect me in the least!" Mostly out of fear of being blacklisted, I made my way in, only to find that my assumption couldn't have been further from the truth. For the past 5 days, all I've done is drink, cry, and try to come to terms with the words Liz shared, but more so, the experience that she and I share. I suppose there is another confession I must make before I can divulge my main confession. I pre-judged Liz as an overly chipper, entirely too optimistic philanthropist with nothing better to do than come talk to a group of disinterested students. It wasn't long before I was clinging to every word that left her lips. It rapidly became apparent that she wasn't what I had characterized her to be. No, not at all. She's me. Twenty years older, wiser, and happier, but still, the similarities were undeniable. Like Liz, I too was sexually abused as a young child. While my abuser was not my neighbor, it was the neighbor of my uncle. Like Liz, I too was found out by a written confession of the abuse. Like Liz, I too was disregarded, and the story of my abuse was swept under the rug, not to be discussed again for years. Everything about our stories were almost exactly the same, down to the fact that both of our fathers were engineers. This happened when I was seven. It wasn't until I was twelve that anyone else became enlightened to my secret. It wasn't until Wednesday that I realized that I'm not alone. I was periodically sexually abused on more than one occasion in the years that followed the first incident. This secret has held me captive for nearly seventeen years. I became the poster child for sexual abuse. All of the signs were there without me ever realizing until I began tirelessly trudging down the path to a career in psychology. I suffer(ed) the substance abuse, the sexual promiscuity, the constant mistrust of everyone I've met, and more. I've wrestled these demons for far too long, and frankly, they were winning. WERE being the operative word. Without ever attending a meeting, Girls with Sole has changed my life in a way that perhaps nobody would have ever intended. By just hearing her story and the progress she's made I've decided that it's time to put all my demons to rest once and for all. I've always had this notion that it would be anything but acceptable for a future psychologist to seek psychological counseling. After hearing Liz's uplifting message, and seeing that it's possible to win this battle, I'm finally ready to let that stigma die. I'm going to get the help that I've so desperately needed for almost two decades, and move forward as a happier and more enlightened version of myself. The process starts here. I immediately went out and bought a brand-new journal - a positivity journal - and have started to write three positive things that happen every day. For far too long, I've fixated on the negatives and allowed life to happen to me, rather than being in control of my life and the things that occur therein. I'm no longer the same scared little girl that I was all those years ago. I'll embrace my fears that I've been carrying. I didn't come this far just to fall. From this day forward, I will no longer be afraid, or stuck in a cycle of negative thinking. I'm putting down the wine, picking myself up, and I will climb my way out of the grave I've nearly dug myself into. Liz Ferro has changed my life for the better. I know I have a very long, emotionally tolling and tear-jerking road ahead of me, but for the first time in my life, I'm ready to begin traveling down it so I too can have my "Finish Line Feeling."

"I am willing to put myself through anything, temporary pain or discomfort means nothing to me as long as I can see that the experience will take me to a new level. I am interested in the unknown, and the only path to the unknown is through breaking barriers, an often-painful process." ~ Diana Nyad

Dear Liz Ferro,

I am writing this letter regarding your recent article in "Family Circle," June addition, "A Sporting Chance." I really enjoyed reading your story. It is good to know that there are wonderful people like you that truly are making a change in these young girls' lives, by encouraging them while making them feel valuable in their life, which led me to write to you. I am working on a thesis project for a class that I am taking. The topic is 'Preventing Kids from Entering the Juvenile and Department of Correction System.'

I am currently incarcerated in a women's facility in Florida. The thesis project that I am working on has not only become a thesis report, but it personally hits very close to my heart, because I have two daughters that have been affected by my poor choices.

The statistic rate for women that are incarcerated and then their children becoming incarcerated is 70%.

I want to be able to help young girls, so they don't become part of the statistic rate. I have talked with many women in here; some come from good families while others have little to no family support. The main key that most of us have in common is the lack of love, attention, and feeling some sense of value and validation growing up. Many of us searched for this in material things, like me. Others turned to men and some even drugs. I want to be able to make a difference, and that is why I am passionate about this thesis project.

I know there are many active organizations, yet what we really need are proactive organizations, like yours, making a difference and making an impact in these young girls' lives - it's our future.

Your story inspired me to want to learn more about your organization. I would like to know if you have any material information about your organization, the success rate of the young ladies in your program, as well as any statistical information.

I truly appreciate any information you can send me for my thesis report. I thank you for your time, and I look forward to hearing from you.

Sincerely,
S.F.
Incarcerated in Florida

"People may give up on you but you must never ever give up on yourself." ~ *Unknown*

Liz I wanted to let you know something and I hope it makes you proud. I hope you're proud of me but I really hope you're proud of yourself. I have been facing a lot of depression lately, and although my struggles now may be so much different than they were when you met me almost ten years ago, they still consume me some days from the normal working average life that I try to live.

I want you to know I have felt desperate and hopeless for a while .. last night I hit rock bottom. I just wanted a way out, but I didn't want to hurt anyone.. so I called suicide prevention and they gave me some resources. I spoke with a woman on the phone until I fell asleep. I woke up feeling absolutely the same, though, and even more hopeless like nothing could help.

I have had no idea how to help myself, what to change, where to begin or what I even needed fixed. I still don't know all of that, but thank you. Thank you so, so much for teaching me the first step that I can take...the only one I have ever known to help, and the one I almost forgot actually did. I always felt so strong and empowered and confident in your classes, and it could always put these feelings aside and make me feel worth something.

I finally see a way out Liz and it was when I thought of you when I was crying driving to work this morning wondering how I would push through another day, and I don't know what made me think of you, but now I know how. I'm going to get though my shift today and I'm signing up for a membership to the gym before I go home. I know it won't all be fixed just by hopping on the treadmill but for now it's an escape I'm going to use that you showed me and I do want you to know that I even will probably quote yourself in my head a few times "you're a rockstar" was always my favorite. It made me laugh.

I really hope this serves the purpose I sent it for and not to worry you because I am making my way back to the happy me I know that you know too. (The me you always brought out) I want you to know you're still impacting me Liz you're still helping me without even knowing it you still inspire me to be a better person and I truly thank you for it all. Thank you for teaching me all that you have and for bringing me up when I was down and teaching me how to bring myself up too. You'll never know how much you've helped me in my struggles and you'll never ever be able to be thanked enough for everything you do. You're a rockstar too.

You've helped me so much Liz and everyone needs to know how powerful GWS really truly is, and the courage and strength that you instill in all these girls using the program.

I would never have known an escape from my struggles and wouldn't have found the strength I needed without you showing me I had it. You truly make a difference.

Paige, Age 24

"The question isn't who is going to let me; it's who is going to stop me." ~ Ayn Rand

My name is Shawna and I'm in Residential Treatment and foster care. I'm about to turn 18 and age out. I have a daughter from when my uncle raped me. She's in foster care too. Girls with Sole gives me strength courage and hope. Ms. Liz is my inspiration and she really keeps me going. I love Ms. Liz and the other people she brings to help us.

Girls with Sole is an empowerment group where I can learn coping skills and clear my mind when I'm upset or frustrated. We have a pit bull mascot named Stella, which is beautiful. Ms. Liz is a very sweet woman and no one is there to judge you.

We are all unique and can be ourselves with Ms. Liz. She truly cares for us girls and puts a lot of time into us and she even buys us new running shoes. I don't even think this essay can actually describe how I feel about Girls with Sole and Ms. Liz.

Seriously, and she has been through a lot and achieved everything she has. She climbed to the top. She did it and I can do it too because I believe in myself and nothing is impossible ever. I'm going to be a nurse and have a family and be happy.

Girls with Sole is a place to learn about myself from other people and from moving and exercise. People who are encouraging and feel like a long lost family. Girls with Sole is like a getaway for me where I can feel strong and safe and empowered. Nothing is impossible, only if we believe it is. Girls with Sole tells me I can achieve and I love it.

Shawna, Age 17

• Some names have been changed or omitted for privacy.

PART SIX
INSPIRATION STATION

"A river cuts through a rock, not because of its power
but its persistence." ~ Unknown

Did you think this was the end? Fuck no, rock star! This is just the beginning of what's possible as you unleash your inner superhero! Don't stop yet! Use the final pages of this book to motivate and inspire yourself: doodle, dream, chase goals, and keep track of the ways that you kicked ass on this amazing adventure! We've even included some tips, samples and examples to help ignite your passion and live your healthiest, happiest life.

You can never rock too hard - or too loudly. You're a one-woman revolution! Don't forget it!

Make a list of your own favorite motivational or inspirational quotes. You can quote other people or feel free to make them up yourself!

_____

_____

_____

_____

_____

_____

_____

_____

_____

_____

_____

_____

_____

_____

_____

You have to ROCK before you can roll!

For example, say you want to rock out a 5K - but you aren't sure how to start - here's an 8-week plan that combines walking with a gradual build up to running. Of course, you don't have to do a competitive 5K race, but I find there is no better way to get started and to motivate yourself than registering for a race and putting it on your calendar. Don't let the word "race" intimidate you. Knowing that you have one in your near future will keep you inspired and consistent with your training. Picture that finish line and imagine the accomplished feeling that comes with it! The plan I like for new runners is 8 weeks in length and can be done outside or on a treadmill. In an earlier chapter, I shared Bill Bowerman's awesome quote: "If you have a body, you're an athlete." So, in that same line of thinking, if you can walk - you can run! The basis of this plan is to walk/run at first, and then gradually build into a 30-minute run.

This is a 3-day per week plan - but supplementing with other activities on the "off" days is highly encouraged! Go for a bike ride (or engage in other forms of cardiovascular exercise), do yoga, or do body weight training/circuit training to keep you strong, balanced and to mix things up!

Be sure to listen to your body and adjust the schedule as needed to allow for much-needed recovery time. Begin each workout with a five-minute walking warm-up, followed by a five-minute walking cool down. If you're brand new to exercise, please consult a physician before you start a new workout plan!

The 8 Week
Rock Before You Roll Plan

Week One
    MON: walk 2 min., run 1 min. (7x) = 21 min.
    WED: walk 2 min., run 2 min. (6x) = 24 min.
    FRI: walk 2 min., run 3 min. (5x) = 25 min.

Week Two
    MON: walk 1 min., run 3 min. (7x) = 28 min.
    WED: walk 1 min., run 4 min. (5x) = 25 min.
    FRI: walk 1 min., run 5 min. (5x) = 30 min.

Week Three
    MON: walk 1 min., run 6 min. (4x) = 28 min.
    WED: walk 1 min., run 7 min. (4x) = 32 min.
    FRI: walk 1 min., run 8 min. (4x) = 36 min.

Week Four
    MON: run 8 min., walk 1 min., run 9 min. (2x) = 38 min.
    WED: run 9 min., walk 1 min., run 9 min., walk 1 min. (2x) = 40 min.
    FRI: run 9 min., walk 1 min., run 10 min., walk 1 min. (2x) 2 min.

Week Five
    MON: run 10 min., walk 1 min., run 10 min., walk 1 min. (2x) = 44 min.
    WED: run 10 min., walk 1 min., run 12 min. (1x) = 23min.
    FRI: run 12 min., walk 1min., run 15 min. (1x) = 28 min.

Week Six

MON: run 15 min., walk 1 min., run 15 min. (1x) = 31 min.

WED: run 15 min., walk 1 min., run 18 min. (1x) = 34 min.

FRI: run 18 min., walk 1 min., run 20 min. (1x) = 39 min.

Week Seven

MON: run 10 min., walk 1 min., run 21 min. (1x) = 32 min.

WED: run 10 min., walk 1 min., run 23 min. (1x) = 34 min.

FRI: run 10 min., walk 1 min., run 25 min. (1x) = 36 min.

Week Eight

MON: run 26 min. (1x) = 26 min.

WED: run 28 min. (1x) = 28 min.

FRIDAY: run 30 min. (1x) = 30 min.

At Week Nine or Ten on a Saturday or Sunday: Race Day (Or not - it's up to you!) Revel in the fact that you did the work and YOU ROCK!

10 Minute ROCK Revival Workout!

Do each set-one right after the other. When it starts to get too easy...do the entire list twice.

30 jumping jacks
5 pushups
20 lunges (10 each side)
5 pushups
10 ab crunches
7 squats
5 pushups

1 minute jog in place
25 mountain climbers
1 minute walk or march in place
30 second plank

How To Be a Super Sleeper

Make sure you get enough sleep and don't try to play catch up if you don't. Try for 7-8 hours a night.

Try to go to sleep and wake up at the same time every day.

Be sure to exercise regularly - but not too close to when you go to bed.

Don't watch TV in bed.

Reduce daily caffeine intake - especially after 3:00 pm.

Make your bedroom comfy, dark and quiet - and not too cold or too hot. The temperature of your room makes a huge difference in the quality of your sleep.

Don't eat or drink too much before you go to bed. Your body can't relax properly if it's busy digesting - or if you have to pee.

If sex isn't an option - some self-satisfaction can help as a natural sleep aid - fuck warm milk!

10 Basic Tips to Superhero Health

- Be grateful
- Don't hold onto anger
- Eat clean
- Think dirty
- Exercise
- Sleep
- Get plenty of water
- Crank up the music
- Laugh often
- When in doubt, don't ever stop saying: "Fuck that: I ROCK!"

To get you kick started, and to continue being kickass, track your emotional and physical progress; your workouts; the way you think; and how you feel for each day of the week in the areas below. Try to do this for at least four weeks, so you can gauge your improvement, and see where you still might need some extra effort. :

_____

_____

_____

_____

_____

_____

_____

_____

_____

_____

_____

_____

_____

Sum up the week: How did it go?

_____
_____
_____
_____
_____
_____
_____
_____

How did I feel?

_____
_____
_____
_____
_____
_____
_____
_____

TOTAL TIME I
WORKED OUT

_____

THE CHECKLIST

When you reach the end of something, like this book, perhaps, the natural assumption is that it's over. Finished. Complete. The next logical course of events would be to literally close the book on it, move on and forget about it faster than your last New Year's Resolution. Well if that were the case here, rockstar, it wouldn't fit into the category known as Super, now, would it?! This book - and your newfound surge of superpowers - transcend any old resolution because you are a one-woman ROCK Revolution.

Right about now, I'd bet my last laser gun that you feel you possess the same true, real-life superpowers that I do which are: resilience, optimism, courage and killing stereotypes. They may seem like basic attributes or qualities to some - but those evil arch villains obviously didn't read the book, so why would we listen to them anyway? Clearly, ROCK powers are extremely impactful and super powerful when used consistently. Because of them, I keep moving forward even when I'm afraid. These powers, and my willingness to keep going no matter what, is my leg up and keep my superhero stance strong - even if I feel like the weak nerdy alter ego for a minute on the inside. Metaphorically, my hands are on my hips, with my back straight, and my chin slightly tilted toward the sky, as my cape whips wildly in the wind behind me. Fear will always be a factor...you will never not be scared...but that's not a reason to quit. When you feel self-doubt or fear begin to creep into your mind and heart, that's when you push harder than ever. The people who don't stop and keep moving forward are the ones who succeed. They are trailblazers, rebels and the one-women revolutions who see the possibilities. They recognize that the finish line isn't the end...it's the beginning of what's possible and embrace the fact that they are a work in progress. Being a one-woman revolution doesn't mean you are alone - or that your efforts are solo. You are among an army of other rockstars, who like yourself, are poised and powerful, and who fight to create positive change within themselves and the world. As they say, with great power comes great responsibility.

Oddly enough, there are times when I'm conducting Girls with Sole programs that I simultaneously feel happiness and warmth in my heart, along with the sensation of being punched in the solar plexus. One particular day at a Residential Treatment Center that I work with, while creating paper dream catchers with the girls after our workout, I felt just that. The girls were telling me how happy Girls with Sole makes them - and that it gives them hope for a better life. Then the punch came when one young lady told me that she was in foster care because her dad raped her, but that GWS inspired her and kept her going. She told me that she desperately hoped to be adopted, and she wanted to know if I would adopt her. My heart felt crushed and, although I knew it wasn't rational, I felt like a horrible person because I wasn't able - or in a position - to adopt her.

The lesson here is that nothing this impactful is going to be easy, but one of the many upsides is that I love GWS, and what it's able to provide for our girls. The girls are truly amazing, which is why I felt I needed to do something truly amazing in order to lead the girls by example. That's when I made the decision to Lace Up and run a full 26.2 marathons in all 50 States of America in less than three years.

By challenging myself in this big way, I could show the girls and the world that the finish line is the beginning of what's possible- and that with the power that ROCK gives us, they too can lace up for a lifetime of achievement.

While simultaneously running the Girls with Sole organization, its programming, and a total of 1,310 miles across America, the 50 States For Sole campaign helped bring in much-needed funds to sustain the organization while also creating awareness - but it ended up doing so much more. It was a constant reminder that I was on the right path, and illustrated the direct correlation between fitness and running with the inspiration and power it can bring to other aspects of our lives. We all have our own personal journeys and versions of the Finish Line. Running, biking, swimming, art, reading, movies, animals, nature, music and whatever else we consider as a soul essential are powerful, ROCK-solid reminders to persevere. I believe they are symbols of hope and inspiration for everyone to cross their personal Finish Lines - whatever they might be. This will, in turn, empower others to do the same thing, creating a beautiful ripple effect that can span generations.

In this legion of ROCK Superstars, you must complete the following 10 activities to prove your commitment to yourself, your fellow rebel girls, and to all who will benefit from your powers.

1. Choose your one most dominant Superpower.

2. Choose your Superhero name.

3. Create your Super logo or trademark look.

4. What would your Supermobile look like? Mine is a Ford Escape! (LOL)

5. Get rid of Kryptonite in whatever form that is for you. List at least three negative thoughts, people or things in your life that you vow to eliminate so your powers stay intact.

6. Decide if you will have a sidekick…and create or make note of that person or animal here.

7. Create a list of at least two healthy things that you will do to increase your strength, energy and wisdom.

8. What are three things you can do to help someone that will also move your soul?

9. Set a goal that scares the crap out of you. Execute your plan and accomplish that goal by facing fears, stretching beyond comfort zones, and diving in head first.

10. Do something both physically and mentally that you didn't think you could do, or that someone told you that you couldn't do.

PROLOGUE

When we aren't sure how to start something or approach a difficult task, I always say it's best to just start at the beginning and go from there. This is going to sound like some serious Willy Wonka shit, but I'm going to end this adventure at the beginning as well.

At the beginning of this workbook, I mentioned that for the majority of my life, I was thought of as a lost cause. When I was in my twenties, I taught nine aerobics classes per week at a few different fitness and athletic clubs in downtown Cleveland. At that time, one of my two older brothers worked downtown as well. His office was at City Hall, and his job was the Finance Director for the City of Cleveland. It was the Christmas Season, and since I had a break in between teaching group exercise classes, I decided to buy some cookies and pop into my brother's office to surprise him with them. The administrative assistant told me that my brother was in an informal meeting with the city's Law Director, and to go right into his office. I walked in with my cookies in hand - and a stupidly proud smile on my face because I was in his huge office with the giant desk - all proud of him for his important job - and proud of myself for what I believed to be an overtly kind and warm gesture. Then my brother introduced me to the Law Director as the "Aerobics Queen" and topped that introduction with the quip: "You and I are the directors, and she's the directionless."

In recent years, I brought this scenario up with him, and he said that although he doesn't remember saying it, he definitely agrees that it sounds like something he would say. Who knew that all these years later, I would be able to use what happened to me, the things that were said to me, the way people viewed me, and the way I viewed myself as a way to uncover my inner superpowers that could help others feel like they could find their way to a place of empowerment.

At the beginning of this book, I said that it's all about challenge, passion and change. I am so grateful to have discovered how to use my challenges to grow and change in ways that ROCK! We all go through tough times, so why not use them to help us uncover the passions that can light our souls on fire, and then use those passions to change our lives and the world around us.

When I was born, I was given to the foster care system. After living in four foster homes amongst trauma and abuse, I was adopted at almost three years old. At the age of eight, my next-door neighbor began sexually abusing me and continued to do so for about a year. When my mom discovered what was happening, she made the fatal mistake of sweeping it under the rug. Maybe if we ignore it – it will go away. Well, much like anything that needs healing –ignoring it can often do more damage than good.

For much of my life, I felt helpless and out of control - like I wanted to run away from myself. I wondered if I would ever feel at home in my body. I agreed with everyone who said I was crazy or directionless. In my mind, there would never be a map to help me find my way.

Like a chest full of gold that is buried at the bottom of the ocean, and never unearthed, those memories might not see the light of day, but I'm not ashamed of them. I'm actually glad that they exist because they have become the map to my superpowers, and are a big part of what makes me the treasure that I am today.

The old feelings of self-hate and patterns of self-destruction that were my life for so many years were actually the spark that ignited my passion to create the non-profit, Girls with Sole.

It took a long time, but with the therapeutic effects of running, biking and swimming…I found my way out of the deep darkness and into the blue skies of a life that finally felt free. The heavy weight of self-hate was completely washed away, and I came to the realization that the rest of my life would be dedicated to bringing this same realization to girls who need it.

My whole life I was told I was wild and crazy. This was never meant as a playful or funny compliment - like the two wild and crazy guys played by Dan Aykroyd and Steve Martin on the old Saturday Night Live episodes. When I was young, I had a sizzling energy that, combined with my mistrust of the world, and my inner anger...created a neutron bomb of wild behavior ready to go off at any given moment. I was prone to sudden, angry outbursts that were beyond alarming to those who witnessed them. I was always considered "too much" of everything that was unacceptable. I was too loud, too wild, too sensitive, too destructive and disruptive, too obnoxious, too talkative, too moody, too crazy, too much of a perfectionist, too hard on myself and others – just "too much!"

Thank God, I kept running and swimming, and it was both these things that kept me from turning to drugs and even from suicide. I knew I was "wild" and that people worried about me and for my well-being. Sometimes, I was even a little afraid of me, if truth be told.

For most of my life, being a wild and crazy girl was considered a bad thing. Therefore, in my mind, I was a bad thing. I became a people pleaser and desperately wanted other people to like me so that I might like myself. I desperately hoped someone would help me recognize that I had at least one redeeming quality.

The quality that was unanimously recognized by all was that I was athletic. I took this and literally ran with it. I nurtured it because it made me feel whole, awake, and alive! My body and brain thanked me graciously. In sports, taking chances and pushing things a little too far is considered a good thing. You can channel negative energy into something so rewarding and productive. I found an answer to my apparently questionable, yet unanswerable behavior that boggled so many minds.

I quickly recognized that athletics and fitness made me feel special and could do more for my mind and body than therapy alone could ever accomplish. Being an athlete was the superpower that helped ease the pain of repressed childhood sexual abuse and built my strength both emotionally and physically.

Today, I realize that being a wild and crazy woman – an authentic and thriving version of the girl that scared so many – is a very good thing. I'm still my wild and crazy self...but I have honed my prowess of fiery energy and learned to channel it in a positive way. I have decided to use my powers for good, instead of evil. (Insert a giggle here.) Girls with Sole does this for our youth. It provides them with the fundamental tools to believe in themselves; to love themselves; to be fit and well in mind, body and soul; and, like me, to take great pride in their wild, one-woman revolution status. Once you harness this power and use it wisely and in a healthy way, you can accomplish anything. The girls in Girls with Sole quickly begin to learn this lesson – the lesson that took me over twenty years to figure out for myself.

Today I'm too happy, too energetic, too helpful, too loving and caring, and too wild and crazy...in all the best ways possible!

Focusing on challenge, passion and change - and using it to ROCK isn't easy... but we all have the choice and the power to rise up from the dark depths of pain into the light. Oftentimes, on our way out of the murky darkness, those same things that hurt us become our superpower that we can share with the world!

"The door is more than it appears. It separates who you are from who you can be. You don't have to walk through it....you can run." ~ Franklin Richards, The Fantastic Four

Never, ever forget that you ROCK- and always share your superpowers with the world!

RESOURCES THAT ROCK

Like a true Rockstar, you don't want the party to end - and I don't blame you. Living a Super life is pretty amazing stuff, and not only can it go on indefinitely, but it can also continue to keep you energized, entertained, encouraged, enlightened and empowered!

Check out this Super list of 10 apps, blogs, and websites that ROCK the house!

1. Girls with Sole.

WWW.GIRLSWITHSOLE.ORG and @girlswithsole on Instagram

> This is the proverbial "no-brainer." I hope you will continue your adventure with Girls with Sole and check in to see what we're up to! You'll find lots of quotes to inspire you, get some fitness and wellness motivation, and maybe see a pic or two of cute dogs.

2. Greatist

WWW.GREATIST.COM

> This blog is awesome because its topics are funny and entertaining, while also educational and empowering. The articles are the real deal and offer inspiring information in areas of health and fitness, moving your body, stimulating your mind, and even finding a new, healthy and affordable recipe to try.

3. Rich Roll Podcast and Blog

WWW.RICHROLL.COM

> I dare you to listen to this podcast and not be enlightened. Rich Roll is an amazing ultra-endurance

athlete, vegan, author (and so much more) who really knows his shit, but also does interviews with the top fitness and wellness leaders about a wide variety of topics. He has a super engaging style and brings out the best in everyone he interviews - just when you thought these superhuman couldn't get any better!

4. Trained by Nike

We talk a lot about the benefits of training and working out in this book. Nike's podcast is all about training and brings you up close and personal with fitness leaders and superhuman athletes alike. You may think these folks never have an off day, but Trained by Nike keeps it real and gets the pros talking about the days that they aren't feeling it - in a "celebrities are just like us" fashion. Sometimes, it's nice to know that it isn't just us mere mortals who don't feel like working out and need an extra push to get through the tough workouts! If you want motivation as well as some great tips on focus, mindset, and endurance topics...check this one out.

5. Black Fitness Today
WWW.BLACKFITNESSTODAY.COM

Ilen Bell and Lauren Bell are a fantabulous married couple who founded Black Fitness today: an online magazine and blog. This dynamic duo strives to make an impact in the fields of health and wellness in the African American Community and to showcase African American fitness professionals who might otherwise be overlooked in the media. They cover topics such as training, recovery, motivation, nutrition, and do amazing interviews with the pros!

6. Anacostia Yogi - Yoga for the People

WWW.ANACOSTIAYOGI.COM

I can't express how incredible and fabulous this Washington D.C. Yogi and blogger is - so you'd better go check her website out for yourself! She refers to herself as a "modern-day revolutionary tackling health disparities in her own unique way and teaching wellness in her neighborhood of Anacostia." I'm pretty sure she's the epitome of a one-woman revolution who ROCKS.

She's a wealth of peace, power, health, and healing - and living proof that a one-woman revolution can have real-life superpowers that, when shared with the world, make it a better place.

7. ESPNW

WWW.ESPN.COM/ESPNW/

Seriously? Hello! This one is a given for all women who ROCK! Prepare to be inspired by words from pros and emerging athletes, exciting sports coverage, intriguing interviews, as well as lifestyle and culture.

8. Rock My Run

This app truly rocks because it keeps you in step and on track - and it's tons of fun! You can pick your seamless mixes done by professional DJs and then rock your run by setting the tempo to whatever cadence you want to maintain - or - have the music mimic your heart-rate or the speed of your foot strikes. Never get bored on a run - or with your music - again.

9. Streaks

This ingenious app turns the things you want to make a daily habit into a challenge that keeps you bent on not breaking your streak. If you have a competitive streak in you, prepare to dominate any healthy habits to-do list you can come up with because this app keeps you in check.

10. Charity Miles

The fact that there's an app that can make you a better, healthier person and help others in the process is simply genius. This app tracks your movement and then donates to the charity of your choice for every mile you log. I truly feel that this app is Super awesome, even though I wasn't able to get Girls with Sole on their list of charities. But that doesn't make it any less amazing, and I love it anyway. Definitely check it out if you want to feel good while doing good at the same time.

PERSONAL NOTES

50771886R00080

Made in the USA
Middletown, DE
27 June 2019